THE INNER
CRITIC

A Practical Guide to Understanding and
Overcoming Conflicts of the Mind

Montriel V. Jamari, LMFT

BALBOA.PRESS
A DIVISION OF HAY HOUSE

Balboa Press books may be ordered through booksellers or by contacting:

Balboa Press
A Division of Hay House
1663 Liberty Drive
Bloomington, IN 47403
www.balboapress.com
844-682-1282

Because of the dynamic nature of the Internet, any web addresses or links contained in this book may have changed since publication and may no longer be valid. The views expressed in this work are solely those of the author and do not necessarily reflect the views of the publisher, and the publisher hereby disclaims any responsibility for them.

The author of this book does not dispense medical advice or prescribe the use of any technique as a form of treatment for physical, emotional, or medical problems without the advice of a physician, either directly or indirectly. The intent of the author is only to offer information of a general nature to help you in your quest for emotional and spiritual well-being. In the event you use any of the information in this book for yourself, which is your constitutional right, the author and the publisher assume no responsibility for your actions.

Any people depicted in stock imagery provided by Getty Images are models, and such images are being used for illustrative purposes only. Certain stock imagery © Getty Images.

Print information available on the last page.

ISBN: 978-1-9822-4599-3 (sc)
ISBN: 978-1-9822-4600-6 (hc)
ISBN: 978-1-9822-4601-3 (e)

Library of Congress Control Number: 2020916900

Balboa Press rev. date: 05/05/2020

To my mother, Shelia A. Thomas-Moore.
Without her, it would not have been possible
to be who I am today.

Special thanks to Michelle Beltran,
for your continued support, critical eye, and
especially your warm heart, which is so appealing to
all who are fortunate to be a part of your life.

"What makes your writing style stand out from other self-help authors is the sincerity of your approach. It's enthralling. You do not attempt to write as a psychological professional; rather, you write as a psychological caregiver who has been a victim of negative past experiences and has overcome these circumstances. You write as a mental hero.

I cannot help but give a positive review for the intelligence and sincerity of the book. It's ultimately satisfying, touching, and filled with beautiful personal and nonpersonal stories.

As the first person to read the book, I must say, 'good job' to you for a well-thought-out title and inspiring content. It's been an honor."

—Editor

Everything on the earth has a purpose, every disease an herb to cure it, and every person a mission. This is the Indian theory of existence.

—Mourning Dove Salish

CONTENTS

FOREWORD

In a fractured age, when cynicism is god, here is a possible heresy: we live by stories, we also live in them. One way or another, we are living the stories planted in us early or along the way, or we are also living the stories we planted— knowingly or unknowingly—in ourselves. We live stories that either give our lives meaning or negate it with meaninglessness. If we change the stories we live by, quite possibly we change our lives.

—Ben Okri, Nigerian storyteller

As I reflect on my thirty-five-year professional tenure as an educator, trainer, and supervisor of counselors—in particular, marital and family therapists—a number of students have been memorable. Montriel Jamari is certainly one of them, and our relationship has continued well beyond our tenure at university.

Early in Montriel's graduate program as a marital and family therapist, we began our journey together. Each Thursday like clockwork, he would arrive at my office door, standing stoutly and sporting a contagious smile along with his welcoming baritone. I would learn quickly that these visits were not the protocol of a student seeking curricular assistance. Our relationship was not born of convention, but of kindred spirit. Our weekly discourse was characterized by family and personal stories nested in the cultural, the racial, and, at times, the spiritual.

I was drawn back in reflection on these visits as I began reading *The Inner Critic*. It was not because the stories were familiar—almost all of the stories, in fact, were surprisingly new—but rather because the style and method of Montriel's presented ideas invited a depth of personal introspection relevant to the message at hand.

As I began reading, it was as if I were again in my office, sitting with him and together creating adventure and sometimes even finding resolution. I do believe readers of this book will unwittingly journey into their own relationship with the author as well. Monte, the name used by his friends, opens this work with a vivid narrative that takes the reader along the landscapes of the development of his own inner critic, beginning in Salt Lake City as a young boy and eventually leading him to Africa as an adult. As he weaves in and out of evocative descriptions and spontaneous cherished memories, I believe readers will find, as I did, that the path of the inner critic gives way to concepts and lessons applicable to humankind at large—we can see our own journey, at least in part, in Monte's. His trip back home ultimately ends in a grandson's promise realized and, perhaps by extension, yours.

Subsequent chapters then cleverly use inspiring quotes, enlightening parables, and particular tropes that spur readers to form their own associations and connections amid life's obstacles and trappings, subject to the surveillance of the internal critic in both positive and negative ways. For each dilemma, Monte offers a way around by encouraging readers to take a stand against these intrusions and disruptions. The voice he brings through his writing resonates with us, as though our minds are one in a stream of consciousness.

The Inner Critic guides the reader through the theme of one's inner critic with simple yet profound questions. Monte is a storyteller who has scribed here a message of mental health by means of oral tradition. The words offered are in themselves a self-journey for the reader, a healing journey on which the author's inner voice serves as guide.

At its end, hopefulness lives on. The reader is gifted with historical references that set the tone for the book, and the rhetorical nature of the questions posed sets in motion self-reflection, contemplation, and a vehicle toward ontological resolve. The anecdotes and examples provided propel the reader to aspire to a more virtuous life and a more elevated moral character.

Monte has mastered the therapeutic use of epigraphs, metaphors, and folklore to steer the reader's reflective journey, and he closes with a set of guiding virtues, a moral map to follow, a means to balance spirit, mind, and body to reclaim and maintain one's rights over writing their own life story. He makes such good use of epigraphs, in fact, that he inspired me to open this foreword with what I believe is a relevant quote for this text as a whole. Monte has a story to tell, and he tells it well. Enjoy the read.

—Arthur R. Sanchez, PhD

CHAPTER 1

My Own Inner Critic Experience

When one door of happiness closes, another opens; but often we look so long at the closed door that we do not see the one which has been opened for us.

—Helen Keller

As an eight-year-old boy, springtime in Salt Lake City, Utah, was particularly memorable to me. Our cherry tree was in full bloom, bursting with pink and white blossoms, and our backyard was soaked in the aroma of jasmine flowers. On the other side of the fence next to our house, the open fields looked like an artist's palette, brilliantly dotted with yellow chrysanthemums, lavender lupins, orange daisies, and softly creeping buttercups. Distant lawn mowers humming in the air created a sort of harmony as grass was cut for the first time after a long, cold winter.

Some of my favorite memories are of playing with my baby sister in the front yard on our Big Wheels. In the morning, before we headed out for those adventures, we would take in our usual dose of

Saturday-morning cartoons. There I was, in my favorite red and blue Spider-Man Underoos, sitting downstairs on our brown shag carpet.

After breakfast, my little sister would bring her favorite doll downstairs, sit next to me in her beanbag chair, and ask, "What are you watching, Bee-bomb-bow?" That was how my sister would say my African name because she couldn't pronounce Odihambo.

"I'm watching that funny rabbit," I'd explain. In one episode, the main character took a trip to Africa. We laughed wildly at what seemed to be a harmless and hilarious kids' show. My imagination would then run wild in our backyard. I often took my GI Joe and Transformer toys on imaginary trips to the distant lands of Africa. They would face the mighty lion and other fierce animals of the African continent. I made a superhero cape out of my sister's baby blanket and flew to our tree house in our backyard. Up there, I imagined overlooking the landscape of the Serengeti. I envisioned the silhouettes of the acacia trees and plumes of dust from the migration of the wildebeests. I saw an enchanted land of wonder and mystery.

Where Did I Come From?

As a youth, I felt a burning desire deep within to understand another part of myself in relation to Africa. Into adolescence, I wanted to be proud of my heritage, but I didn't know how. I learned a little about the origins of my ancestors from TV series like *Roots* and *Shaka Zulu*. This was my first exposure to a small part of African culture, and it only piqued my interest more.

I was taught a bit about Africa in middle school and high school, but I never quite understood why learning about this vast and dynamic continent didn't play a larger role in mainstream education. Although there was little discussion or time devoted to a place that comprises one-fifth of the earth's entire land mass, I do have a clear recollection of sitting at my desk and seeing references to the "Dark Continent" in my assigned textbook. That sounded so ominous and bleak, not just mysterious and unknown, but scary even. The study of Africa was a blur. Why did we spend so little time exploring the antiquity of this intriguing country and so much time on the European empires, their colonies, and their influence on modern-day culture? Why was the Western world so highly valued and brought to light while my homeland was so neglected and cast in shadows?

All these questions left me feeling frustrated as a young American student because I got the impression that Africa and, by extension, its native peoples were insignificant. Dispensable. A commodity. A resource. Surely, there were African impacts on literature, art, poetry, technology, architecture, science, and math, not just European ones? So why weren't we being exposed to *those* influences too? It all felt deeply dismissive, frustrating, and insulting to me. When I'd leave class, I remember feeling angry and embarrassed. I didn't even want to look at my classmates because I simply felt ashamed.

The Birth of My Inner Critic

In *The Souls of Black Folk* (1903), W. E. B. Du Bois describes a phenomenon called "double consciousness"—the fallacy of seeing and judging yourself through the eyes of another. He talks about how American Negros would see themselves through the eyes of their white counterparts and judge themselves according to that psychological measuring tape. They could never live up to the standard they aspired to because they would be limited by the thoughts, opinions, prejudice, and bigotry of others. Du Bois goes on to discuss the splitting of the psyche:

> Two souls, two thoughts, two unreconciled strivings; two warring ideals in one dark body, whose dogged strength alone keeps it from being torn asunder.

I have discovered that this phenomenon of double consciousness is universal to all humans. Think for a minute about the people *you* feel watched and judged by, how you see yourself through *their* eyes. These perceptions often give rise to various internal feelings that actually have external roots, such as anger, anxiety, depression, irritability, and confusion. In essence, you feel like you are being controlled by something outside yourself.

This double consciousness started taking hold of my thoughts and gave rise to my inner critic in several ways. Quite early in my life, many disparaging beliefs and questions began to emerge and move to the forefront of my thoughts and behaviors, among them:

- Black Americans are different.
- Black Americans were fighting a losing battle.
- Did Black Americans' unique physical, cultural, emotional, spiritual, and intellectual qualities have significance?
- Black Americans seemed powerless to change their fates and futures.

The frustration I felt began to affect me in more ways than one. The frustration turned into anger, and the anger gave more power to fear. As this inner storm of frustration, anger, and fear began to take shape, I developed an inferiority complex. Over time, I became aware of its destructive nature. I didn't want to contribute to it further or become a casualty of the psychological damage it was causing within.

By the time I was in my early twenties, I'd come to a crossroad and needed to make a decision about my future. In the calm that exists in the eye of a storm, I gained some clarity on what direction I wanted my life to go in, on who I wanted to be and how I wanted the world to view me. The veil began to lift, and I realized what was required to create effective change: I needed to travel to Africa, to see it for myself and feel the deep soul connection I'd always had with the continent. It was there that I would explore and hopefully reconcile the unfinished business of my inner critic. To begin the journey of silencing, or at least negating, the negative inner voice that had been steadily growing inside me throughout my youth, I knew I had to understand the meaning of my African culture, lineage, oral history, and folklore.

I Dream of Africa

My father came to America in the 1970s as an eighteen-year-old foreign exchange student on a scholarship. He was from Mfangano, an island on Lake Victoria in Kenya, and my mother was from Carthage, a rural town on the east side of Texas. They met in California on the Chico State College campus and began dating after much persistence from my father. They would have three other children besides me (all younger). Unfortunately, their relationship did not last, and they parted ways when I was very young. I have some memories of my father before the breakup, but they're only bits and pieces.

During my adolescent years, I developed a strong curiosity about my father and where he came from. I knew something was missing from my self-understanding, and this sense of lack was pulling me toward a burning desire. It was almost as if a circle needed to be completed or a void within needed to be satisfied. I wanted a firm grip on my concept of "maleness," to know how to act as a young man. I was envious of my peers who had their dads there to support them at father-son events.

But I also felt drawn by something more powerful and more salient than an understanding of who my father was. It was that soul connection I've mentioned, and it went beyond just my relationship with my father. I believed then and I still believe now that his forefathers were calling me back home to Africa to discover who they were, to hear their voices, and to walk on the black sandy beaches they walked on before they set sail on their fishing excursions. It felt important for me to traverse the same mountainside my father did on his way to school, the same trail his father traveled to meet with his fellow elders to discuss the affairs of their people. My ancestors were calling me to walk the beaten paths of the beautiful island of Mfangano, and until I did, I knew, my soul would be left wanting.

My mother and my aunt Sarah (my father's cousin) were two of the greatest influences on my desire to travel to Africa. My aunt would tell me vivid stories of how brave my paternal grandfather was, how he faced a mighty boa that had attacked a young child with a makeshift spear and shield he fashioned from a rusty, abandoned car bumper. He was recruited into the English army and survived World War II. He donated land to the community for subsistence farming.

All these stories were part of the legacy he left behind, but my aunt would say that the stories could only go so far and that I needed to experience and author my own story. I needed to go claim the land my grandfather gave to me as part of my birthright. I needed to leave behind a legacy for my own children, for the people of Kenya I'd meet, and for the people I'd work with throughout my planned career as a therapist. This wouldn't be my whole story, but it would be part of my story. And it wasn't just about the land; it was about my connection to it. I needed to claim who I am as a person, my mother and Sarah always urged me—not from what I'd heard in the media or in books, but from firsthand experience.

I received my passport and my Kenyan visa in the mail. When I saw the iconic shield and spears of the Kenyan flag, I was extremely excited. I knew my lifelong dream of traveling to my homeland was going to happen. Maybe not immediately—I still needed to save up more money, which wasn't easy because I was paying my way through college at the time—but it was going to happen. When I finally had enough funds, I bought my ticket to Africa in fall of 2004.

My Kenyan family was elated when I sent them the news. They told me they were very proud of me for taking it upon myself to go there and meet the people. My grandfather especially could not wait for me to come see the birthplace of my father. I was my father's firstborn and my father was my grandfather's firstborn, and there is a special relationship that exists within African culture with the firstborn male child. I am also the firstborn of all my Kenyan cousins, so I have inherited that responsibility as well.

My Journey Home

Africa has been loved, feared, and misunderstood throughout the centuries. It has been ravished by famine, war, pestilence, and intertribal conflict, and it has been conquered by imperialistic foreign countries. Many of these countries came to Africa to take the resources and the bountiful wealth that the land has to offer. The indigenous people, particularly on the east coast of Africa, were part of this bounty. To this day, Africa is controlled by governments that are not necessarily for the people. They are more interested in personal financial gain and comfort. This reality is evident by the disparity between the rich and the poor and the haves and the have-nots.

But from the sky, I couldn't see any of this. From the sky, I looked out the airplane window as we began our descent and saw only an enormous sun setting on the horizon, like liquid gold being poured over an endless savanna. I immediately felt a sense of newness and connection that transcended all my fears. And moments later, when we touched down at Jomo Kenyatta International Airport, I immediately felt at home.

Luggage in tow, I met up with my aunt Serina, who happened to work in the airport and who had arranged to come collect me. She'd been so eager for my arrival that she'd taken time off work to greet me and had been waiting for my plane to land for hours. She introduced herself with genuine affection and asked *"Ithi nade?"* (How are you doing?) in her native Luo tongue. She joyfully escorted me through the various security barriers, taking all of the stress out of the customs process for me.

Everything felt so surreal as we made our way through the airport. The language of the people all around me fell on my ears in a natural poetic cadence. It was the language of my soul, and I felt it quieting my inner critic. Why was it becoming silent? What was it about this place or my presence here that was quelling my self-doubt, the constantly murmuring negative voice I'd grown so accustomed to at the back of my mind? Was it because I'd chosen to challenge the critic with this display of courage, confidence, and faith? Because I was facing my fears and confronting my questions head-on instead of staying safe back home in America, safe in my routine, surrounded by who and what I already knew?

Looking back now, I know I was emboldened during this first pilgrimage to Africa because I was doing something by myself, for myself. It wasn't easy—I recall being afraid of the unknown and wondering if I would be truly accepted by my father's family. Thousands of miles away from all that was familiar to me, what would happen if I were stranded? If I encountered episodes of civil unrest or scenes of civil war? If I got lost or attacked? Preparing for my trip, I'd done my due diligence by studying the social climate of Kenya, but the truth is I knew very little of what to actually expect. I just took a leap of faith and trusted the draw that I'd felt within. I didn't let fear consume me or my worries alter the path toward my goal. I simply felt a calling from somewhere beyond, and I answered it. To this day, I believe that it was indeed the heeding of my soul's higher calling that marked the turning point in vanquishing the voice of my inner critic.

The next voice I heard in reality, however, was that of my uncle Ellie, my father's second-youngest brother, who'd made the fourteen-hour trip from Mfangano Island to the airport in Nairobi to pick me up. His English was good, but he wished it was better, he told me, so he could clearly express how happy he was to see me. My uncle Kwasi, a finance director for the local government, lived in an upper-class neighborhood in Nairobi with his family, and so Ellie and I stayed at his house for a couple of days, eating the traditional African food that his wife prepared for me. Then Kwasi set up transportation for us to the island.

The trip from Nairobi to Mfangano passed through the highlands and the African savanna. Going through various small towns along the way, I had the chance to see what life was like for the native people across the land. I was bewildered by government-issued luxury cars traveling through slums and paying no mind to the suffering children. It was clear to me that greed, mismanagement of funds, and the dictatorship were influencing the affairs of the government. Society was swallowed by corruption and was in shambles. Most people were dependent on agriculture. Along the road, vendors sold fresh fruit and vegetables. Most of them were trying to make a living on the few shillings they received from tourists and locals.

Ellie and I stopped to enjoy a meal at a small restaurant in Kericho, a big town in the highlands west of the Kenyan Rift Valley. The town was known for its lush forest, agriculture, and tea plantations. Ellie ordered the same thing every time we stopped to eat: a chicken-based soup, the local staple of *ugali* (a cornmeal cake), and a Coke. I could tell it was a special treat for him to dine with his nephew from America. He took great pride in telling everyone we met about me, with his head held high and a smile plastered over his face. I loved spending time with him and was so grateful that he was my companion during my initial trek through Africa.

I was amazed by how many people he knew along the way. He was a well-loved pastor who had a meek spirit and who was very kind to his congregation. He brought a sense of comfort to people, and I could tell they trusted him. He seemed to be especially popular with college-aged kids. I learned that they would hang out around his house and ask difficult questions about life and the Bible. He had a good understanding of the welfare of the people and was well connected to the heartbeat of village life on the island. His connections fascinated me. I saw many similarities between us in our approaches to building rapport and working with others. Later in my life, when I was talking about this time with Ellie, a dear friend said something that hit me on an emotional level. He would be gone one day, she reminded me, so these memories of him should be cherished. "It was good that you gave him the opportunity to venture out with you and have those experiences with you," she went on to say, "that you took the time to enjoy those moments with him. Because in this life, nothing lasts forever." I learned as much as I could from him.

Finally, we approached Mbita, a small, bustling town on a small peninsula on Lake Victoria. Merchants lined the dusty streets. The murmur of commerce was mixed with the baying of goats and cattle. After my uncle haggled with the boat captain for a reasonable price for our passage, we hopped aboard a pastel-colored pink and blue boat. Sitting between a goat and a big bag of rice, I couldn't help but feel a slight nervousness in my stomach. I knew the boat was overloaded with people and commodities, and I prayed, *Please, God, don't let this boat break in half in the middle of the lake!* My uncle must have seen the apprehension on my face, because he looked at me, smiled, and said, "Don't worry." When someone tells me not to worry, it usually has the opposite effect, but here in my father's homeland for the first time, I wasn't my usual self. The confidence and empowerment I'd felt since arriving had stayed with me, and I managed to let go, relax, and trust Ellie's words.

As we headed off, I was excited and curious. I was mesmerized by the sunlight that danced off the waves. The boat was slow, but it was strong and sturdy. As we passed the island Barack Obama's father is from, we came upon a majestic scene that I could never have imagined. I'd had a picture in my head of what my father's home would look like, but it didn't come close to what I was now viewing with my own eyes. The giant fig trees that lined the island looked like they were from prehistoric times. Lush green foliage and exotic animals inhabited the visible spaces. Large groups of native vervet monkeys could be heard in the trees and walking down paths. Black-chested snake eagles were feeding their chicks in huge nests. Otters, weaver birds, and giant monitor lizards speckled the diverse island, making it one of the most unique ecosystems in the area.

As the boat sailed past several massive boulders with exotic birds perched on them, I saw my ancestral homeland in all its glory for the first time. It was like a religious experience. "There it is!" *Pinedala* (the motherland), the locals call it.

About fifty yards from the shoreline, I could see people waving from the beach. As we docked, a short woman in front took my hands and greeted me in her native tongue. She was my grandmother, Dani. She didn't speak much English, but I could tell she was very pleased to see me. Still holding my hands, she said, "Welcome home." I was next greeted by my grandfather, Janedus, my father's youngest brother, Ogango, and several of his kids.

Village Life

The friendly village was a small agricultural and fishing community. Tropical foliage surrounded the open plots of farmland. As we meandered down to the trails, everyone knew everyone else. I could make out some of the conversations, like Ellie saying, "He is the son of Atunda." And the villagers would reply, "He has honored his father and grandfather by coming to see the people."

As we traveled toward the mountainside, my uncle pointed out acres of land that belonged to the family, which my grandfather had inherited from his forefathers. We went to the east side of the island, to Kwitone, to visit the rock art there. These fantastic geometric paintings were made by Twa hunter-gatherers between two thousand and four thousand years ago. Up until the 1980s, it was a site for folklore, rain worship, and connecting to the ancestral spirits. I learned that people wanted to understand their connection to the universe and the land that they inhabited. Their form of spirituality was connected to their livelihood and survival. They depended on the seasons and the earth to provide for them and their families.

As I walked into the cave, I saw spiral shapes and images that looked like the sun and the moon. I wondered if this was a way of coping with unseen events and trying to understand profound subjects such as life, death, and God—subjects that mortal beings can never fully comprehend but can only try to preserve and portray in various art forms, like this rock painting.

The next morning, my grandmother greeted me with porridge. The simple dish was made from a sweet millet. After breakfast, she wanted to take me for a walk. We journeyed through the mountainside and down some trails. I was surprised by how strong she was. She couldn't have been more than five foot one and was just under a hundred pounds, but she was full of life. She held my hand as we went through what seemed like an obstacle course. I remember being overtaken by her small, strong, wrinkled hands. I remember thinking that these were the same hands that held and raised my father as a child. As we trekked through the countryside, she showed me the route my father took to get to school. It just so happened that we met his teacher along the way. He and my grandmother talked about the old days and what kind of student he was. He said, "You did a good thing, Odihambo! You came back to see the people! You have made your grandfather proud!"

On the path, we also met up with my grandmother's sister. We were invited to have lunch and tea in her small dwelling. Dani was so proud to show everyone her firstborn grandson from America. Dani's sister also said, "You did a good thing coming back home to see the people!"

The next day, my grandfather took me to a plot of land next to their house. He pointed to where the plot began and ended. He told me this would be my land. I promised him that I would return to Kenya to build my traditional home on the piece of land he gave me, but for now I would build a fence around it. This excited him so much that he rose at three o'clock in the morning the following day to start burning a great portion of the shrubbery to open up the space for me.

Ellie and I took the boat ride back to Mbita to buy some cedar posts and barbed wire. I hired a college kid who was looking to earn some extra money to pay for his textbooks to help. As we began the work, my grandfather sat on a rock with his staff and watched the fence being built. I could see the pride in his eyes as he witnessed a tradition being passed down to the next generation.

The Story of My Lineage

One night, my grandfather and grandmother were sitting together on one side of the wall of their home. My cousins were sitting at the opposite end of the room on a gray-colored couch with the cushion missing. I will never forget how the room was illuminated by a kerosene lamp and how our silhouettes danced on the clay walls behind us. We had just finished eating a fish stew that was pretty outstanding, after I was able to get past eating the little fish eyes staring back at me.

It seemed the perfect time to ask my uncle Ellie to ask my grandfather about our ancestors. My grandfather thought for a moment, looked intently at me, and smiled. Ellie took a couple of pages from my journal and began to write down what my grandfather was saying. He recounted our family history going back three or four hundred years in detail—all the names of my forefathers.

He began by explaining in a calm voice that our ancestors originally came from Egypt and traveled down the Nile River. They traversed through Uganda, Sudan, then into Kenya, where they eventually settled on Mfangano Island. My grandfather said, "This is where you come from, and this is the history of our people."

It was transformative for me. A quickening in my soul connected me to something that was greater than all the obstacles I had endured thus far and all the difficulties and challenges I had yet to face. It transcended all the racism I had experienced in adolescence. It gave me a sense of why I was there and that nothing I had been through was not without reason. There was purpose in the universe. I was attached to something eternal. The story of my ancestry felt like something that had been written by the hand of God, and in that moment, it became utterly essential and meaningful to me.

That evening, my inner critic became a distant memory, a forgotten whisper. My inferiority complex still tries to resurrect itself from time to time, but I gained a newfound truth between those clay walls that has never left me. The inner critic is not completely gone—no one's ever is, and for me personally, there will always be more work to do to overcome years of being told who I was—but I now had a greater understanding of my inner self, and that understanding has irreversibly changed my life.

With self-understanding—coupled with education, spiritual beliefs, and trusting in one's own capabilities—self-esteem, self-concept, and self-confidence grow. That's what happened to me, at least, and I know it can happen for anyone. I grew into the belief that I could accomplish anything I set my mind to. Everything suddenly made sense. I realized that those who had died in conflicts to make a better life for future generations—all the names my grandfather recited—they were a part of me, I was a part of them, not in the past, but right now in the present. I realized I am a product of people who made it through slavery, people who fought for freedom and civil rights on my mother's side, people who bestowed upon me a rich heritage on my father's side—all of which set me on the path of learning who I am.

Learning who I am ... learning who you are: what a crushing blow to the inner critic!

The Final Goodbye

My first trip to Africa came and went. As profound as it had been, I had to return home to California, to my mother and siblings, to the master's program I was finishing up at the time. But then there was a second trip.

In the winter of 2015, my grandfather sent word that he wanted to see me. My grandmother had passed away. I knew I had to return to Mfangano to pay my respects. When I arrived at his modest home, my grandfather was resting in his bedroom. Clearly, he was not as physically strong as the last time I'd seen him. After sixty years of marriage to Dani, it seemed like a part of him had gone with her. His wife had been laid to rest to be with her ancestors.

When it came time for my visit to end, I said, "Grandpa, it's time for me to go back." He looked at me and began praying. He started to cry and asked me to "stay forever." I promised him I'd be back again, just as I had before, but he continued to cry and pray. Ellie told me it was the first time he had ever seen his father show that type of emotion.

A week later, my grandfather passed away. Everyone told me how proud they were that I had fulfilled my grandfather's request before he crossed over to meet his ancestors. I had felt a calling to pull back the layers of my selfhood, to discover my origins and my ancestors, to understand how they had influenced the inner critic born in me years ago. Now, with my grandfather's passing, with all my experiences on the island, I felt equipped to carry on the legacy he had passed to me. It felt like that unfinished circle was now complete, was now whole. I felt whole.

Looking Back to Go Forward

My story is uniquely mine and it has led me to where I am today, but we all have a unique story—one that is yours and only yours. We all have things that compel us, insecurities that plague us, lessons that teach us, people who shape us. Growing up as a typical American kid in the late twentieth century, I had no particular tie to Africa. Apart from the color of my skin and news of abuses and atrocities on the continent that would appall anyone, I had no particular reason to journey there early in my life, to meet family members who were virtual strangers to me, to seek out more than I already had.

And yet I was drawn to the land of my father's people with a fervor and focus I couldn't deny. I was fascinated by African history, by its array of mythology, folklore, rituals, written customs, and especially its oral traditions, passed on by elders to their progeny. It's a place where later generations still learn by listening and then by being passionately committed to preserving these teachings by handing them down to still-later generations. These powerful aspects of African culture attracted me, spoke to me, and wove together the fabric that became an understanding of my inner self.

I don't believe that my specific realization is one that everyone needs to have. Everyone's journey through self-exploration is individual unto themselves. And yet it *is* the journey that's important. For every single one of us. We must strive for insight and clarity on our inner beliefs and our outward behaviors. We may sometimes give in to struggles we are experiencing on the inside, yes, and this can cause disruptions in how we are perceived and experienced by others. But it's important to recognize that the filters erected in front of us—by our ancestors and our parents, by our life experiences and hardships, by our culture and our cultural identity—do not always allow us to see objective reality. Some of our behaviors and beliefs come from the outside—our upbringing, our family unit. But no matter where they come from, no matter where or how your inner critic was birthed, we do have the power and control to shape our own lives, to discover our own culture identity, to wipe the fog from our lenses, and to quiet the critical voice inside the mind that is really just another filter erected for our protection.

My journey to the distant lands of Africa guided me down a path that helped me discover a part of myself that affected not only my personal growth, but my professional trajectory, by strengthening my style of psychotherapy. That initial early curiosity about who my dad was led to my desire to connect with his side of the family, which in turn led me to the idea of life's meaning, the greater good, the altruistic value of helping others, and a connection to God. I knew that this connection, understanding of the inner self, and integration of people from different backgrounds all needed to exist on the landscape of my life if I was going to be fulfilled and skilled as a psychotherapist.

Where will *your* journey lead? Where is *your* life path calling you? What needs to be fulfilled within *you*? Are you allowing your inner critic to deter you from your destiny? From your wholeness? Nobody can walk the path for you; it is something you have to do yourself. But many people become afraid, and through fear, they become paralyzed by disbelief. They do not want to venture out on the quest that lies before them. This causes many difficult dilemmas that fuel unrealized dreams: complacency, mediocrity, excuses, victimization, and stagnation of the soul. And these patterns lend themselves to reoccurring themes I have seen over and over again in many of my clients: regret, anger, bitterness, uncontrolled fear, guilt, blind arrogance, and self-esteem issues—all of which make it increasingly difficult to look in the mirror. Allowing these themes to churn in your subconscious mind gives the negative inner critic psychological power over you.

The intent of this book is to help you regain that power by setting you on your own path, by working through the obstacles that are blocking it, and reprimanding and correcting the mental voice that tells you who you "should" be and what you "can't" do. The whole point of telling you my story has been to introduce you to your own— your own one-of-a-kind narrative. We all have different perceived deficits, unfulfilled yearnings, incomplete dreams, unfinished business. Perhaps you don't know who your parents are or were abandoned by one of them. Perhaps you've suffered abuse. Perhaps past trauma has stymied present growth. Perhaps you're ruled by your inner child instead of your adult self. Perhaps you've been dealt some tough cards in your life and have grown weary of playing the game. Perhaps you're just not where you want to be yet. The possibilities of life's disappointments and challenges are literally endless. But just as your specific hurdles are uniquely yours, so too is the way you choose to confront and resolve them, to uncover an enlightening and freeing self-understanding, and to seek your own truth and find your own power.

This book is my story. You are the author of your own. The pen is in your hand. Be brave enough to start writing a story that is different from the one others have told you about yourself. Be brave enough to start right here, right now, with me. Your journey is waiting for you to discover it. Let's embark, shall we?

CHAPTER 2

Your Inner Critic: What It Is and Where It Comes From

A Native American elder once described his own inner struggles in this manner: "Inside of me there are two dogs. One of the dogs is mean and evil. The other dog is good. The mean dog fights the good dog all the time." When asked which dog wins, he reflected for a moment and replied, "The one I feed the most."

—George Bernard Shaw

The nature of the inner critic can be difficult to understand—where it comes from, why it's so pervasive and elusive at the same time. Why does it seem like a whisper on the wind, a fleeting thought pattern we'd miss if we don't pay close attention to it? And yet why does it have such an immense impact on our lives? How can a thing that can be neither seen nor touched be so powerful? And how is it able to change the course of our lives? The inner critic exists outside diagnosable mental disorders, such as schizophrenia and depression. It is not some type of psychological phenomenon that requires medication or long-term therapy to extinguish it. It is a part of us.

The inner critic is the voice we hear from time to time (some of us more often than others). It can be helpful in some ways, like when it quietly warns us that we're about to do something foolish or when it pushes us toward excellence when our will fades. The inner critic can be the quiet guide that gently leads us. But it can also be destructive and hurtful. When it feeds on our failures and mistakes, its persistent negativity can create intense anxieties and feelings of inferiority. It can even turn us into monsters.

The negative form of the inner critic is not gentle. It preys on embarrassment, failure, unhappiness, and fear. It turns them into a dark force that can drag us under the floor—unless we take actions to stop it.

Negativity becomes a cycle when we allow the dark form of the inner critic to take precedence over the good form. One failure can become the source of several other failures: *You failed your nursing program's final exam; therefore, you will never become a nurse. Therefore, you will never be able to achieve the level of financial and career growth you dream of. Therefore, you will never become a good mother. Therefore, you will be an average person, earn an average income, and live an average life.* The failure of your final exam can be regurgitated within your subconscious, fed into your mind, and make you think and act like a *failure.*

Many people let a failure in one area of their lives lead to failures in other areas. A man who has failed in his first two business attempts and has lost investors' money will unwisely allow this failure to enter his marital life. The business failure will turn him into a bad husband and father. When we see this type of life pattern, the negative inner critic is at work in men and women.

The inner critic can influence the quality of our lives and how we view ourselves. It can be a positive influence when it pushes us toward achieving our goals and making sound life decisions. Sometimes, it motivates us and cheers us on in our life ambitions. *You can do this. Don't let that one setback at work get in the way of going after that promotion.* At other times, it holds us back and makes us fearful to pursue our dreams. *You can't do that. You're not capable of that. What makes you think you deserve that?*

The "good" voice of reason is sometimes termed the *conscience*. The conscience speaks subtly when we are about to cut in line or tell a lie. It speaks more clearly when we are unkind to others. It chides us when we spend time partying instead of studying. It speaks loudly when we take something that does not belong to us. Consequently, it lets its voice be heard whenever we're about to do something we shouldn't be doing and when we ignore something we should be doing.

A conflict is created in our minds between the voice that pushes us toward happiness and fulfillment and the voice that pushes us away from happiness and fulfillment. It's just like the caricatures we've all seen of the devil on one shoulder and an angel on the other. They are both telling you what to do, and both hold sway over you. Even though they are heavy influencers, the decision is ultimately yours.

This book aims to guide you toward quieting the negative aspect of the voice that criticizes and heightening the positive aspect of the voice that inspires. To accomplish that, we first need to understand where the inner voice comes from and its level of influence on your life.

Psychological Theories of Origin

Theories of consciousness, subconsciousness, and unconsciousness have been discussed for ages by philosophers, mathematicians, psychologists, scientists, and more.

In *The Sophist* (360 BC), Plato argues that there are three parts of the psyche: the appetites, the spirited or hot-blooded part of the psyche, and the mind, which he calls the "nous." The appetites are simply our desires and pleasures and the things in which we find comfort. He also refers to the appetites as the physical satisfactions that humans seek.

The spirited or hot-blooded part of the psyche is the motivator for overcoming obstacles in our lives. We see this strongly in athletes, for example. Think of Michael Jordan's will to win at any cost or Muhammad Ali beating his opponents through psychological warfare, hard work, and raw talent. The "sweet science of boxing" gave Ali the confidence to believe that he was unstoppable and that he was the "greatest of all time." This is the power within us to persevere through all odds. It is our willingness to take on challenges that seem insurmountable, but also the day-to-day challenges we all face.

The mind, or nous, is the conscious awareness that we have deep inside us. It is the part of us that is rational, that analyzes situations before acting upon them.

In *"Sigmund Freud's psychoanalytic theory of personality posits"*, Sigmund Freud, in his psychoanalytic theory of personality, proposes that consciousness is everything that exists inside your awareness. The subconscious (or preconscious) is the part of your mind that you are unaware of—it is information you are not actively aware of at any given moment, such as thoughts, feelings, sensations, but things that are accessible to you nonetheless with a little focus and effort. The unconscious, however, refers to the part of the mind that resides deep within you—automatic thoughts, programmed habits, urges, deep-seated emotions, traumatic and forgotten memories—that have been repressed but that heavily influence your beliefs and behaviors.

Swiss psychiatrist and psychoanalyst Carl Jung both built upon and digressed from Freud's personality theory. For Jung, the conscious mind is named the "ego," and the unconscious has two layers: the personal unconscious, consisting of dormant and repressed memories (but closer to the surface than in Freud's version), and the collective unconscious, a repository of shared memories from and with our ancestral and evolutionary past—the things inborn in us purely by being human.

These are very simplistic summaries of traditionally and widely accepted theories of the mind's constitution, but they all point to the underlying assumption that there are things we are and are not aware of, things we do and do not have control over, things that shape us and things that we shape. And these aren't just theories—practical applications of psychology of the mind enter into our lives every day in every way. Here's an illustration, for example, of the preconscious mind (more akin to Jung's personal unconscious) at work—the storehouse of memories that are not top of mind but that can be drawn into consciousness at will, like playing hopscotch in kindergarten or being sent to the principal's office in first grade:

I remember seeing a documentary on Tiger Woods. When he was just a young boy, his father was teaching him how to swing a golf club in the basement of their home. Little Tiger was sitting on a stool with his legs dangling as he looked intently at his father's swing. Earl swung, hitting the ball into a makeshift canvas that he had devised to capture the impact of the ball. The club did not make good contact with the ball, thus pushing the ball to the right. Earl asked Tiger what he thought of that swing. Tiger looked at him sheepishly and just smiled. Earl smiled back and said, "Yep, that was a boo-boo!" Later in his son's career, Earl would say, "You know, sometimes we don't give our best swings, and it doesn't go as planned, but in life, we have to just keep on swinging."

Now, these particular comments by Earl are likely not in Tiger's conscious mind all the time. But whenever he makes a "boo-boo" on the course, I'd be willing to bet that he retrieves that memory and that, whenever his stroke fails him, Earl's statement reminds him to "just keep on swinging." The voice in our mind comes even more into play the greater the stakes. When Tiger hit very rough patches in his life—episodes of infidelity, a very public divorce, career-threatening injuries—they no doubt challenged his beliefs in himself. His inner critic would have been on high alert, megaphone in hand. Surely the negative aspect of his mental voice chastised and lamented; but Earl's voice, which Tiger would have internalized after decades of his father's coaching—surely resonated as well, and louder, or Tiger would not have been able to go on to achieve what no other golfer in history ever has.

We can't all be champion players, but at some point in life, we will all face obstacles that threaten to overwhelm us. Sometimes, those obstacles come in the form of choices we must make, choices that will greatly affect our fates. This is when we will call upon the voice that has been developing inside us for all our lives; if we don't call upon it, it will call to us. There are words and images and recollections and scenes implanted in the mind, and once planted, they cannot be erased. They can be analyzed, addressed, confronted, conformed, managed, honored, and heralded, but they cannot be eradicated from existence.

To answer the question of where the inner critic comes from, it can be argued that it stems from experiences and memories found mainly in the subconscious but also in the conscious mind. Our consciousness cannot actively store *all* the information we take in, but bits and pieces can be filed away in different levels of the preconscious—just like our social security number or mother's birthday—can be retrieved when needed. The inner critic is one such "folder" of the mind's filing system. We can recall a father's words, like Tiger Woods, for decades, maybe not verbatim, but certainly the spirit of the message. And our own words, our own voices, come to the fore just as often, sometimes critical, sometimes complimentary, but all arising from one's personal history of incoming and outgoing observations and information. The voice we hear at any particular time or in any particular circumstance not only can but does steer our decisions, actions, and inactions.

Research into the brain and the mind is wide and diverse, but it's agreed that we all have that voice within that draws from positive and negative experiences, from relations and interactions with others, from successes and failures. To understand the impact of that voice, we must consider the different factors that influence the inner critic: (1) relationships; (2) environment; (3) communication; (4) childhood; and (5) the self. The next chapter will explore each factor in detail.

NOTE: As we venture forth in this book together, I strongly encourage you to bring a journal along. We'll be exploring some case studies—some theoretical, some factual—all intended to lead you to your own case, where I'll pose questions for you to ponder, situations that I hope will inspire you to contemplate your own. As you do so, record your answers and thoughts in your journal; I promise you it will serve as a valuable and enlightening companion along the way.

CHAPTER 3

Influences on the Inner Critic

Don't be pushed around by the fears in your mind.
Be led by the dreams in your heart.

—Roy T. Bennett

As with anything else in the human experience, the inner critic does not form in a bubble—it is not an independent, autonomous, finite creation that exists outside of your corporeal being; rather, it is interdependent with your psyche, a flexible and fluid invisible essence that wafts in and out of your mind, a sometimes subtle, sometimes aggressive mental companion that is intimately attached to who you are and how you function in this world. As mysterious and ethereal as that may sound, certain traits and trends of the inner critic are more concrete in nature and solid in substance. The factors that influence the voice of the inner critic—its cadence, tenor, temperament, and refrains—are quite firmly understood and clearly recognized ... and so specific to each individual as to be universal to all individuals. We'll start with the biggest influence of all, our relationships with other people, which will receive the most attention in this chapter on the basis of the tremendous role they play in our psychological development and, therefore, in the development of the inner critic who faithfully accompanies us through the life journey.

Influence #1: Relationships

People affect us more than we think they do, more than we'd care to admit. The effects aren't always visible—lodged in various recesses of the conscious, subconscious, and unconscious minds—but we can trace and observe them through our behavior patterns. To put it simply, you are shaped by the influences of others; whether positively or negatively, there's no escaping the influence others exert on you.

I remember walking with a friend and associate on a college campus. We were talking about books, and the word "library" came up. I happened to say "li-berry," and he then turned to me and said, "It's *library*." I felt so embarrassed. From then on, I never mispronounced that particular word again, and yet insecurity about my English remained in my subconscious.

I worked really hard to try to speak the proper English—not an easy goal to accomplish when you're someone who grew up in a poor neighborhood. I hadn't been exposed to correct diction, and I knew I would be at a social disadvantage if I didn't use proper grammar, since we're typically judged by the way we speak in social settings.

I was determined to turn that a wish into action because wishes are fleeting and not totally useful in the real world. You can wish for something for your entire life and never see it come to pass. In fact, this way of thinking often leads to disappointment, anger and regrets. Putting a wish into action by consistently and dutifully working on daily, short-term, and long-term goals, however, can turn it into a reality. But the negative side of the inner critic doesn't want you to do that for yourself. The negative inner critic wants to convince you that your inferiority is real and that your insecurities are justified; in this way, it keeps you safe in a cocoon of avoiding failure. If you don't try, you can't fail.

I fought that negative side by listening to great orators like John F. Kennedy and Dr. Martin Luther King Jr. I listened to countless debates between people with differing opinions and theories on controversial topics. I listened to people who had beliefs that were different from mine, and I looked at how they reasoned and put together their words to defend their positions. I became interested in debates from the great thinkers of the past. I was fascinated by how they used language to influence others and defend their position or express how they were feeling. Even when I did not understand everything they were saying, I did not give up on trying to learn and process the information. I looked up the words that they were using, how to pronounce them and their proper context. You might get discouraged and then give up too soon when something hard or embarrassing comes your way. Remember that the mind needs to be challenged in order for true, lasting growth to take place. Embarrassing moments are opportunities for this to happen.

In church, I worked on writing sermons and looked at myself in the mirror as I was speaking—sometimes getting up at three or four o'clock in the morning to practice. I would self-critique my hand gestures and body movements as I began to deliver my main points to the imagined audience. During this time, the voice of the negative critic would say, *You're fumbling over your words. They're going to think you're dumb.* But the voice was quieted as I gained more confidence because I did the *opposite* of what the negative voice was telling me to do. The more I put forth valiant efforts to get better, the better I became. What are the words the negative critic is whispering to you? Are you doing the *opposite* of what the negative voice is telling you? What kind of work are you willing to put in?

Along the way, people encouraged me, and that became a motivating factor for me to keep going. Eventually, I was able, through hard work, to speak in front of hundreds of people at a time. Many people were helped by the messages of hope and encouragement I imparted. If it had not been for that one embarrassing moment with my friend on that college campus, I would not have had the same amount of dedication to challenge myself to conquer my insecurity about public speaking.

Encouraging Words Along the Journey

Motivating words from others—their force cannot be overestimated. There was a tiny, elderly Black woman in church. Mama Dixon couldn't have been much over five feet tall, but she was a powerhouse. She wore a little black round hat, pointy rimmed glasses, and a simple black dress to match her black shoes. She sat next to the wall heater during Sunday services to keep herself warm. I was just a young boy at the time, and I loved to be around elderly people, particularly her.

I went through some hard times during my childhood. It was difficult to talk to people about the hardships I was going through. But it was almost as if Mama Dixon had insight into what I was experiencing. She would call me over from across the church, look me in the eye, smile, and say, "Son, you just keep being encouraged. God has something special for you! Don't give up!"

Long after her peaceful death, her words of faith still rang true within me when things were challenging. When that inner critic starts to censure and castigate, Mama Dixon's words—now embedded in my soul as deeply as, if not more so than, that critical voice—combat the critic, tame it and quiet it. Her positivity in real life overrules the negativity in my head, and this can apply to anyone, anywhere. Yes, our relationships with others can plant seeds that allow the negative inner critic to grow and thrive, but they can also plant seeds that blossom into a fuller, more dimensional view of ourselves than we alone can see from our subjective perspective.

Who in your life encourages you? What words do they speak to you that resonate in your mind and implant in your heart? Write down who and what comes to you in your journal. We all need someone who reinforces our efforts at personal growth. As social creatures, we need good people around us to objectively validate, critique, and advise us on the actions we want to take. In fact, research has shown a direct correlation between a decrease in depression and a combination of diet, exercise, and being socially active with *positive people*.

When people pass along encouraging words to us, I believe that's the true voice and hand of God at work—inspiring us when we feel dejected or alone in life. And when our lives ultimately end like Mama Dixon's, we are not remembered for how much we acquired during our lifetimes; we are remembered for the lives we have changed for the better. Not only can you and should you embrace encouragement when it comes to you from any source—granting it the power to conquer the negative critic—but think about the impact your own encouragement to others can make as well.

Discouraging Words and Actions

What personal insecurities do you remember having or still have in your life? Think about it for a moment. Do you still remember the sight, sound, smell, and colors of those experiences? It is difficult to divorce ourselves from memories and relationships of the past that have shaped our self-esteem and self-concept. Many of the choices we have made in life are the direct result of how people thought about us. How profound is that! So often, other people's insecurity, resentment, anger, jealousy, abuse, and fears are projected onto our own lives. Let that sink in for a moment. Their "unfinished business," as it's sometimes called, has deeply impacted us. Their own thoughts and experiences motivate how they have chosen to parent, guide, and, as a result, shape us. Take this time to write some of the names of these people and their impact on your life in your journal.

The unanswered questions that reside deep within all of us likely arose from early experiences. Questions like: *Why didn't they want me? Why did they leave me? What did I do to warrant such meanness or neglect?* Typically, issues of abandonment stem from the experiences we had with our primary caregivers. These issues often haunt our adult relationships and contaminate the idea of true happiness with the person we choose to be our significant other. Some people will choose a partner to fill a void within them, putting undue pressure on the individual and the relationship. This leads to serious problems down the line as the relationship matures from the honeymoon period to the everyday reality of facing a parade of challenges. You cannot hide from yourself. You cannot cover up the *unfinished business* and expect another person to heal you. Later on in this book, we'll discover ways of managing this inner conflict.

For now, suffice it to say that internalized negative themes of insecurity that originated early in our lives leave no room for rational thought. It's like there's a constant tug-of-war within, an ongoing inner struggle that complicates your life more than they need to be. Rational reality is pulled under by irrational beliefs that lead you to feel like you're never going to be happy, that you don't deserve happiness, that you're never going to be good enough. If we do some investigating, we find that these thought patterns date back to times in our lives when we wish we'd made different choices; remarkably, some of them might even date back to generations before us—to people far back in our family tree who wish *they'd* made different choices and then unknowingly passed on their regrets and disappointments and ingrained thinking patterns to their offspring. In this case *you*.

This discussion brings to my mind a man named Jim Kink, who struggled with attention deficit disorder. When he was nine years old, he overheard a teacher saying about him to another faculty member, "Oh, that's the boy with the broken brain." Can you even imagine the effect this had on a young boy? Think back to a moment when you heard a negative label or story about yourself. How did this affect your self-confidence? How long did you carry this message with you? How has it affected your relationships with others and the choices you have made in your life? Does it still affect you today? Capture the memory in your journal now and, in hindsight, explore its lingering effects.

The Challenge of Stuckness: The Story of the Chicken Man

Another by-product of our relationships with others in terms of how those relationships feed the negative inner critic is what I call "stuckness"—not just the things that happen to us in our lives that stymie and stall us, but how others react and respond to our life events in turn. Motivational speaker Les Brown tells a story about when he was a congressman in Ohio that aptly illustrates this dynamic.

During his lunch breaks, Brown would go out in front of the capitol building in Columbus to just people watch and enjoy the outdoors. He recalled one person who was there in the square each day for everyone to see. The children and adults thought he was humorous and entertaining. They would laugh at him and his antics. He was known as "Chicken Man" because he had a feather in his hat and dressed like a chicken.

Chicken Man would drive downtown with a chicken on top of his car, occasionally blowing his horn and blinking his lights. He would walk downtown pushing along a baby carriage with two baby dolls in it. He also carried a picture of a woman holding two dolls. When anyone approached, he would screech out a sound just like a chicken makes. Most people would laugh at Chicken Man, not knowing his story, which was this:

Chicken Man woke up at three a.m. one morning to the blare of an alarm. His house was engulfed in flames and smoke. He panicked and jumped out the window. Then he heard his wife and children screaming for help. He ran to the door to go back inside, but the flames were too hot. He desperately tried to get back into house, but despite all his might, he could not. Soon, the cries for help stopped. His wife and two little girls perished in the house fire.

When Chicken Man's brother-in-law learned that his sister and little nieces had died in the fire, he grabbed Chicken Man and began beating him violently. In utter agony, through his tears, he yelled, "Why didn't you save my sister! You're a chicken! Why didn't you save them, you chicken! You saved yourself! You're a chicken! You're a chicken!"

When people pulled the brother-in-law away from Chicken Man, they asked, "Are you all right?" Chicken Man looked at them and began to make the sounds of a chicken. Chicken Man no longer had the use of words, could only make the sounds of a chicken from that point forward. He never spoke again. The tragedy was so severe that he became stuck—a classic example of post-traumatic stress disorder that triggered psychotic features. But the townspeople in the square each day didn't know this; all they saw was an eccentric guy who clucked and squawked like a chicken and traveled around with dolls.

There is always a bigger picture and a greater story behind what we see on the surface. This man who people laughed at and thought was crazy or entertaining had a tragic history underlying his behaviors, a history in which he was stuck. He was drowning in extreme guilt, and his mind had scripted a very dark story of who he was. His brother-in-law served as the catalyst for the man's altered mind patterns, but once they'd been altered, he accepted and assimilated them.

What can you come away with from this story? Trauma can be a vehicle for *Stuckness*. Possessing an understanding and knowledge of why and where your trauma comes from can give you a heightened sense of power and control over your life. When you become aware of the origins of your belief system—whether positive thoughts or negative ones—you have the potential to become the master of your own thoughts and behaviors. You are the gatekeeper of your well-being. You may be challenged at times by the trauma you have experienced, but it need not control you or dictate your life choices negatively.

You are the author of your own story—at all times. You no longer have to cater to the changing tides of someone else's interpersonal flaws and baggage. You don't have to be the beneficiary of your caregivers' perceived beliefs about who you are. At this time, you are whole. Exactly as you are *right now*.

The negative inner critic would have you believe you need more in your life, however—that you are not whole, that you're lacking somehow. This thought pattern is the compounded effect of your past experience; it leads you to believe that you are broken or insignificant and that your voice does not matter. We may have been told these untruths by the voices or actions of our caregivers and others who had a profound effect on our developing years, and perhaps still do. As a result, you may have sought out ideals or an illusion of happiness, not true happiness.

We tell ourselves, *If I can just make a million dollars, then I will be happy and people will respect me. If I can just show her my value, then she will love, care for, and accept me. If I can just graduate from college, then I can show him that I'm.... not... dumb.* The logic behind this type of thinking seeks to fill a void, mostly out of fear, insecurity, uncertainty and wanting to be validated. There is nothing wrong with the desire to become a millionaire, to be loved by someone important to you, or to push yourself toward excellence. The problem arises when we seek validation through a *perceived* desire from someone else and not our own. Metaphorically speaking, this is the nagging itch in the center of our backs that they refuse to scratch for us. This relinquishes control over our lives and indirectly gives away our power to another person or persons. There's a difference between striving for self-improvement and the idea of trying to fill an empty void in our lives—it can be a subtle difference at times, but there is a distinction.

You often find ourselves wondering why. The question of why is the natural end product of the progression of thought as you try to make sense of the abuse or any other painful experience that was inflicted upon you at an early age and may even be continuing now. As hurtful as these memories are, you do not have to live in the pain of them; you do not have to live in insecurity and uncertainty.

It is important for you to make a conscious choice to live, think, and behave differently. You do not have to be persuaded by the pressures of the negative inner critic as it attempts to get you to believe that something about you are missing, wrong, broken. It takes work—it's not an easy thing to free yourself from the captivity of the past and make lasting change in your thought patterns and behaviors. But it can be done. You *can* get "unstuck."

Consciousness: The Case of the One-Eyed Blind Man

Traditionally, the motif of the one eye is a metaphor for consciousness. When our consciousness is foggy or even blinded, our way of seeing the world is limited and skewed. We see only one way, much like black-and-white thinking. Our lives are shaped and colored by our past experiences and highly influenced by the way our parents raised us, their personal cultural mores, religious beliefs, moral codes and values, how they communicated with each other, and how they attach to others. Our upbringing obviously instills a type of bias in us as we navigate the world. The conflict arises because this bias is not always correct.

A client of mine, Todd, is representative of the allegorical one-eyed blind man. He's granted me permission to share his experience, and his name has been changed to protect his identity. His story is significant in that it captures this dilemma of childhood trauma that can blind a person to behaviors that create great pain for themselves and others in their sphere.

Todd entered my office for the first time somewhat suspicious of therapy. From the moment I met him, I could tell he was guarded. I did feel a certain connection with him, as I was able to receive and accept him for who he is. I could see his potential and the pain inside him. There was a dark corner within him that was filled with dust and had not yet been explored. It was littered with fear, doubt, uncertainty, and a lack of trust of the people and the world around him.

Renowned psychologist Carl Rogers says the best way to exemplify empathy with the person sitting across from you is to receive the whole person, what he terms *unconditional positive regard*. As Todd sat in the chair opposite me, I deliberately practiced this positive regard as I started to pick up on his nonverbal cues. His glance would veer off to the right, he'd look down at times, avoiding eye contact. He would ask a few questions about me and where I came from. As he began to feel more comfortable, Todd naturally began to talk about his story.

Todd's mother was an alcoholic. She struggled with her sexuality and her experiences with men. Her young son became the object of her anger, often representing the men who had violated her. When Todd talked back to his mother at six years old, she reached into a drawer and picked up a hammer. In her rage, she threw the claw end of the hammer at Todd's tiny body. The hammer barely missed his head and struck the wall behind him. In deep fear, he ran and hid under his bed. With tears running down his face, Todd asked, "Why?"

This question would follow him into his adult years, slowly building up into anger, resentment, and distrust of others. He described a switch he felt inside—he was never the same after that episode. He sat in my office, continuing his story with a cold, indifferent tone, taking occasional glances up at me. He told me about his destructive behaviors, of his alcohol abuse and of the pain he felt from time to time in his liver.

It was a challenge to connect Todd with his own feelings. I knew it was necessary for him to connect with the hurt, pain, and feelings of abandonment if he was to progress forward in his life, but these feelings were suppressed deep within him and overshadowed by thoughts of violence and self-harm. The question of why lingered, haunted him, and accompanied him into relationships with people who truly loved and cared for him. It was easier to push those people away because he could control the trust that way. He didn't have to risk being vulnerable with them.

Unfortunately, Todd's story of childhood abuse didn't end with his mother, but followed him into foster care, where he had poor attachments with his caregivers. He was eventually kicked out of the system because he "aged" out as he put it. Thereafter, Todd found himself getting into trouble and having deep resentment in his heart. He projected his anger onto others. Consequently, he often got in fights and resorted to violence as a way of coping with the fear of abandonment.

Todd's inner critic told him that he had no worth. That people would eventually leave him or betray him. That he could not confidently trust anyone. To live in this emotional pain was like reliving the abuse from people he trusted. That there was nothing to live for. What is the purpose of going on this way when the future is so dark and bleak? His past experience would blind him to the reality that he did have value and indeed his life was worth living. He wanted to die.

Even amid our darkest hours, some light will break through, and in Todd's case, he did find one counselor during his time in foster care who was very helpful and who changed him forever by providing guidance and offering a new perspective that Todd had never considered. Through this one nurturing relationship, Todd got a taste of what trust could mean, what unconditional love and acceptance could feel like.

But past demons are hard to conquer, and later in his life, Todd would find solace in the same vice that robbed him of his mother, often drowning his pain in drunken stupors and blackouts during which he wouldn't even remember his own abusive behavior toward his wife.

Todd's story encompasses several major tenets of one-eyed blindness. First, he was seeing the world from a defeated viewpoint, which he learned from his mother. Essentially, he was modeling her coping mechanisms. He was echoing her story, which read, *I can't trust anyone.* He learned to falsely believe that anger was the answer and that he was unlovable.

Todd's experience shaped his mind to the extent that he began to believe trust and attachment to others were things he did not deserve. He suppressed his desire to connect with people in order to protect himself from feeling the pain of abandonment. This kept him from being vulnerable with others who had no intention of harming him. This created a barrier between himself and others, and he could not create meaningful relationships.

His inner critic manifested in ways that created distance between him and mindfulness, making it difficult for him to stay in the present. This would lead him down a path of constantly making the same emotional errors and never learning from them.

Reflecting on Todd's behavior, when we see others hurting, including ourselves, why do we continue with destructive behaviors? We do this as part of an unconscious defense mechanism to avoid suffering and to defend the one part of ourselves that we are trying to protect. It could be the little boy or little girl in us. We naturally desire to detach from painful experiences by giving ourselves to these destructive self-deprecating behaviors. The irony lies is our willingness to go through suffering, to embrace it, to stop avoiding it but to instead learn and grow from it.

Instead, we end up cheating ourselves out of, experiences that would grant us deeper insights into who we are as self-sufficient human beings. Pain is a great motivating factor to learn about the real world and how we ought to navigate through it. In Todd's case, he was living in the past, haunted by memories of people who hurt or violated him. The ghosts should have been exorcized out of his life, but they remained lurking in the halls of his inner house. Like a poltergeist that terrorizes a family from time to time with its ominous presence, the past can plague us and paralyze us with fear. Many people try to escape their fears with alcohol, sex, drugs, or work. People in Todd's life were witnessing how his ghosts were haunting him in the form of his behaviors and attitudes toward life, family, and himself. The accompanying anger that he expressed toward his family and society made it difficult for him to love and to be loved because of the fear of being vulnerable, insecurity, the lack of trust and uncertainty. What ghosts are haunting you? Do you hear the banging down the hallways of your emotional self? Are you terrified to look in the rooms that have been locked for some time now?

Only once he was willing to work through the past and be present in the here and now could the veil of darkness begin to lift—the veil that had blinded him to parts of reality by limiting his sight. In therapy, we worked on no longer suppressing his past hurt but instead letting it come to light, airing it out, and in the process of exploring it, he started to see where his anger and suicidal thoughts were coming from. He began to heal as he talked through the issues of abuse. His mind naturally unraveled the complexity of emotions and rational thoughts. He was discovering the value of his supportive wife and children.

As he was becoming more emotionally available to his wife, they were bonding in new and meaningful ways. They discovered fun and spontaneous sex, raw laughter, safe communication, and precious moments of feeling heard. He created a deeper connection with his wife and, in turn, increased intimacy.

Likewise, Todd's children now trust him as a father. His older daughter especially can open up to him, communicate freely, and feels safe when discussing her feelings. His new connection with her kept her from being bullied. He listens more than yells. He is setting an example of how to communicate with his family in a loving, purposeful manner. During family meetings and interactions, his kids see the change in their father and are proud of him and want to be around him.

Now, all this takes hard work and consistency. There is always the temptation to fall back into old patterns. You are not going to achieve these results by being inconsistent. You will not achieve the goals you set out to complete in life if you neglect to do the work it takes to venture down the path that includes hurtful experiences. These experiences are our teachings, and the way through them is where the deep healing happens. Some might argue that we need not look to the past—that it just steals more time from our present. In some cases, this may be true. However, the past can be a great teacher and if the past is seeping through in a way that hinders your life, it must be addressed.

Your experience in life may shroud the eye of your consciousness by fear, uncertainty, insecurity, and the fear of abandonment, like Todd's was. But your experience is something you can learn from without suppressing it—allow your learning from your negative experience be the lens through which you see your unique qualities and value. Many people are blinded by the veil of the past that covers our inner eye; that keeps us from seeing our true and valuable self.

From this perspective, we cannot see all the opportunities in front of us, our resilience, our fortitude, and the people who truly love and care about us. These experiences are what characterizes your unique qualities.

The Fear of Vulnerability

Todd's story naturally flows into a discussion of one of the greatest motivators in his past experience: the fear of being vulnerable to the hurt that others can inflict on us. In both my private practice and my own life experiences, working with others has helped me realize just how many people are terrified of vulnerability. As a result, they exhibit behaviors intended to protect them from it. This does not help them in their relationships with others because the lack of vulnerability is the exact opposite of intimacy. Clients often express their concerns to me that their significant other is cold, distant, unresponsive, and unwilling to meet their emotional needs. It is virtually impossible to be in a loving relationship without being vulnerable with the person with whom you are involved.

Let's explore this basic human need of vulnerability. What does it mean to be vulnerable? Is it really a type of weakness or an act of surrendering one's power to another, as many people believe? I think the reverse is true; I think vulnerability is a commendable strength.

I've felt vulnerable many times. I recall leaving one-sided conversations with others that I deeply trusted. I remember feeling defeated, feeling a tremendous load on me after talking to people that I thought truly care for me. I would often wonder why rather than feeling better having opened myself up to them, that I actually felt worse for having confided in them, sometimes just by being near them. I eventually realized that I was internalizing their negative energy, fear and unprocessed issues. When others project their unresolved or unfinished business on us, it's a breeding ground for the inner critic to take center stage. The internal dialogue that emerges fuels insecurities, and in my case, that took years to overcome. I'd become lost in self-doubt and uncertainty when exposing myself to others led not to their support, but to their criticism of my actions, and that criticism steered my personal narrative.

But the irony is that I wouldn't trade that experience for anything! It helped shape who I am today, and it was a fantastic opportunity to learn about a greater part of myself. Without risking being vulnerable with others and the coinciding emotional distress that sometimes caused, I would not have gained the insights I have—insights that changed me. For the better. This idea of openness to vulnerability ... it's the whole reason I included my personal story in chapter 1 of this book, the reason I chose to open the book that way: I'm asking you to go on a journey with me, part of which entails exploring some potentially dark corners of your psyche, so I decided to share my own journey first—to explain my own background, to narrate how I came to concentrate on the inner critic, to expose some of my own dark corners along the way. If negative energy comes my way as a result of that, then so be it. I had a reason. I was willing to be completely open. The positive aspect of my inner critic encouraged me to approach this book that way, and since I've learned to listen to that voice over the negative aspect, I choose to believe that my vulnerability is a strength that will be worth the risk—not just here, but in all parts of my life as I help people along their path.

As you discover more about yourself, you, too, will have to make a choice about how you are going to receive the negative energy of others when you display vulnerability with them and it backfires on you. Will you use that to your benefit, as a teaching moment? Or will you choose to absorb the negative energy as if it's your own, as if it can defeat you? When someone mistreats your vulnerability and mishandles your trust in them by failing to give you what you were hoping to receive from the interaction, that's actually on them, not you—that's their issue to work on. In my experience, it's always better to continue to risk honest communication with others than to retract into a shell and hold yourself back from genuine connection.

Vulnerability can be your friend in your relationships—it makes a real difference, and here's why:

- It builds trust.
- It builds a greater sense of empathy.
- It invites acceptance of the other person using unconditional positive regard.
- It opens you up to love.
- It builds resilience in the relationship.
- It builds a greater connection to God or a higher power.
- It allows you to become more forgiving of yourself.
- It encourages being more honest about what you believe and feel.
- It takes a nonjudgmental stance.
- It keeps you from hurting others.
- It creates a space in which you are free to work on personal issues together.

Still have your journal handy? When you've been vulnerable with others, has it worked for you or against you? Can you think of someone in your life with whom you're always comfortable being vulnerable? Someone whose connection with you might deepen if you attempted more vulnerability? It's a fear many people share, but only by exploring your own openness to being more open can you reap the very real rewards of closeness that vulnerability brings.

Silencing: The Case of the Girl with the Silent Voice

I often come across the phenomenon of *silencing*. Silencing occurs in relationships with abusive caregivers, spouses, or partners. It happens when one person in the relationship feels as though their voice is not valued. It is the constant belittling of being told that what we say is stupid or dumb or selfish. We are laughed at for expressing our thoughts or opinions. We are told to be quiet. After being treated this way just a handful of times, the script is written and then repeated in the subconscious—it's the dialogue of the negative inner critic—and it becomes the manual of how we construct our lives. Needless to say, this has a tremendous effect on self-esteem.

I worked with a young lady in my practice—we'll call her Cheyenne. She came into my office in tears because of the constant berating by her father. This sweet young girl was full of promise and wonder, but her path had been fraught with adversity. Child Protective Services was a part of Cheyenne's life from a young age. She was sexually abused by her father and other men who came to the home. Her mother was heavily addicted to drugs and emotionally unstable. Cheyenne felt no semblance of love, security, or protection from her parents. Wild parties were a normal occurrence, even on weekdays.

As one would expect, the effects of this home situation were emotionally devastating to Cheyenne. She was diagnosed with ADHD, and her school performance was impacted. Her homework was rarely completed. She often went hungry, and the refrigerator was empty. Mostly, she survived on Diet Coke and Hot Pockets. She has a vivid memory of standing on tippy-toes to put a Hot Pocket in the microwave by herself. Her mother was sleeping on the couch from the previous day's drug binge. Cheyenne slept on the cold floor of the mobile home with one soiled blanket that reeked of human and animal urine.

As she grew into puberty, her father began to eye her. He made frequent visits to her bedroom at night. She clearly recalled being terrified as she heard her father's footsteps approaching down the hallway. The sound of the door slowly creaking open echoed in her mind for years. His ominous silhouette in the doorway was stained on her memory. She'd hide her head beneath the pillow, close her eyes, and pray for God's help. *Go away! Please, not again. No more, please!* Her cries went unheard. Tightly curled up in her tiny, cold bedroom, her father lay down behind her. Her fragile heartbeat, pounding wildly, was deafening in her ears.

The innocence of Cheyenne's childhood was stolen. That her prayers were left unanswered would ultimately affect her relationships and her faith in God as an adult. She began to question God's existence. She thought, *If there is a good God out there, how could he have allowed this to happen?* Cheyenne's journey led her down a path of skepticism and conflicting beliefs. Deep down, she believed in God. But because of her childhood, she began to teeter between agnosticism and atheism.

When Cheyenne could no longer suppress her pain, she sought out therapy. With commitment, hard work, and the courage to venture into the dark areas of her life, she was able to confront the shadow demon of her father. For years, the vision of the dark outline of his body standing in the doorway haunted her. But through her consistent efforts, her father's sins would no longer have a grip on her. Cheyenne learned to quiet the voices in her head, to understand that *she* was not the problem, to rewrite her mental script, and to redirect her inner critic away from self-defeating thoughts and toward self-promoting thoughts. Cheyenne reclaimed her own self-worth.

Today, Cheyenne holds a steady job. She coexists in harmony with the world around her and is no longer controlled by anxiety and fear. Work and family relationships continue to improve even with life's occasional ups and downs. She learned how to drive, received an education in money management, and began saving for her future. She is so proud of herself for setting aside rainy-day money and retirement funds.

In therapy, she sets daily and weekly goals, short-term goals of one to six months, and long-term goals of six months and beyond. She keeps a journal in which she records her narrative, a powerful step in her healing. Each time she makes an entry, she becomes the author of her *new* story. Through writing, she can process her thoughts, feelings, and emotions in a healthy way. She is now giving voice to the innocent, fragile girl in the mobile home.

For your journal: Who has silenced you in your life? Who or what has made you feel unvalued, worthless, stupid? In response, what have you learned to tell yourself—what's your mental script that keeps you locked in a role you never agreed to play? Are you allowing the words of the negative inner critic to govern your actions and beliefs?

There's another option: You can learn to give space to the positive inner critic instead, to allow it to reframe the way you view the world and your circumstances. It's not easy to do—there's no easy way to quell the negative ingrained messages we've been telling ourselves for years, for decades. But if you're willing to do the personal work, you can meet the challenges of life, you can conquer the trauma of silencing, and you can rescript your story so that it is the negative inner critic who is ultimately silenced.

The Past Creeps in Unawares

Why do men often turn out to be what they hate most in their fathers? A boy who was enmeshed in an unhealthy and abusive relationship between his father and mother will often grow up to become an abuser like his father. Raised in such an environment, even though he hated and most likely still hates his father for physically abusing his mother, he nevertheless proceeds to physically abuse his own wife or partner.

This mirroring phenomenon happens when we slowly, over time, incorporate the attitudes and behavioral patterns of the people with whom we have early relationships. We soak in their principles, absorb their ideas, and at times adopt their quirks. Even when we dislike what they do, that dislike can become a bond that defines that particular relationship. For example, if my father is an alcoholic, I can choose to leave that relationship because I can't stand by and watch the self-destruction; I can develop empathy toward people who struggle with alcohol because of my understanding of my father's plight; I can completely abstain from alcohol myself all my life, or I can become my father's *behavioral* twin by mirroring his choices in relation to alcohol abuse. I could become that which I do hate.

There are numerous outcomes in any relationship, of course, and more than one outcome can result. But regardless of which of the multiple outcomes manifest in any given relationship, they often give rise to inner personal conflicts caused by feelings of confusion, hypocrisy, self-doubt, resentment, denial, and more. Such feelings then present as behaviors, behaviors that therefore often have deeper meaning behind them.

The point here is that the effects our relationships have on our inner world do not only occur in the conscious realm, where we know that a particular person's habit is influencing us. The effects often can and do occur in the subconscious realm, where we do not know why we do what we do. The inner voice draws energy from our relationships—good and bad—and subtly feeds us the same energy.

There are many instances of the inner voice coming from subconscious knowledge. Some people instinctively know how to make a happy home. They do whatever it takes to keep their families united. They spread love. They get married and stay married. This instinct is informed by the inner critic, and the inner critic itself stems from experiences long before we're even teenagers. Maybe a sixth grader visited an aunt and uncle over summer break and witnessed the closeness that existed among father, mother, and children, saw the happiness that comes from understanding between couples and patience between parents and children. Many people are raised within the orbit of a loving marriage and learn about it that way—what it looks like, feels like, what it requires to maintain. The effects of such relationships end up existing in their subconscious minds and generate a yearning for a happy home. The inner critic's acquired knowledge subtly tells them to apologize to their spouses when they are wrong. It cautions them when they are taking an argument too far. They don't think about how they know to do these things, they just know it.

Equally, growing up in a rough neighborhood can generate an internal voice that encourages or motivates a person to be violent, often unbeknownst to them. Let's say you lived your formative years in a neighborhood in which you witnessed violent fights on a daily basis. Now you're an attorney, married, with kids, living in

San Francisco. Driving to work one day, a careless driver brushes your car and breaks the side mirror. Instead of responding rationally in proportion to the incident, your inner critic jumps in and tells you to start screaming at the guy and, when he doesn't apologize or take accountability, punch him in the face. You don't necessarily know why you were triggered, you just were. Your subconscious has stored memories of approaching conflicts with violence, of only being acknowledged and taken seriously by raised voices and clenched fists, of getting the outcome you want by forcibly demanding it.

True, your inner critic can also jump in and supply reasons why you should not physically confront the guy—at least not out in the open, where there could be legal consequences. Still, you're raging inside. You see this type of repression in someone who has the expected social restraint in public, but submits to his depraved instincts at home with his wife and kids. Whether he's in control in the courtroom or out of control at home, the rage is there, lodged in his subconscious and provoking him to behave in certain ways based on the anger he learned from his parents or from the fighting masses in the inner city that was his early home. On the outside, people might assume he's an ideal husband with a picture-perfect family, but there's actually a tornado of violence swirling inside him.

Influence #2: Environment

This leads us to the second primary influence on the nature of the inner critic—not just the people who populate our lives, but the places we inhabit, both literally and figuratively, both in the near and the distant past. The voice of the inner critic draws strength from the memories of yesterday or from twenty years ago, and environment plays a huge role in that.

As such, we must be careful of the environments in which we find ourselves stuck: in a bad marriage, in an unfulfilling job, in a dangerous community, in an unhealthy lifestyle of, perhaps, crime or drugs. Living far away from those we love. Having to fight in a war.

Take a look at your life map to identify the places you've been and how those environments have influenced you—what you witnessed there, what you assimilated there, how your mind processed your experiences there and then fed your inner voice by the conclusions you came to. Childhood, high school, college, workplaces, your grandparents', inner city neighborhoods, your friends' homes, trips and vacations to other locales, doctors' offices and hospitals, detention centers, camps—they all present different environments with differing levels of influence on our lives.

Some environmental experiences cannot be classified as either "good" or "bad," just as the inner critic isn't always good or bad. But our past and present environments definitely influence our decision-making, our gut reactions, our trust in others, our sense of obligation, and our precepts and belief systems.

The Environmentally Influenced Inner Critic

Jack grew up in a home where his father was the constant provider and his mother played a supporting role. He went to a good private high school, and so did his brothers. He graduated as the class valedictorian. After college at an esteemed university, he earned his MBA and then got a good job with an airline company. Within two years, he became a junior executive, met Melissa, and fell in love. Soon after they got married, he was promoted to a senior executive position.

This story should have ended happily ever after, but it didn't. When a recession hit, the airline industry was hit hard. Mergers and acquisitions followed. Jack got laid off.

Six months later, he still hadn't secured employment commensurate with his education and skills. Melissa had no problem with the situation. Her job was solid, and the pay was just as high as

Jack's had been. She paid the bills and covered most of their expenses. Until he found a new job, she knew they could get by just fine.

Jack, however, became very uncomfortable with the arrangement. His ego was hurt, and frustration built more each day that he wasn't able to provide. He'd snap at his wife, became unnecessarily irritable and even rude. He sulked on the balcony night after night, eating as little as possible and smiling even less.

Whereas some men would adapt to this situation of the woman being the provider much more readily, Jack's developmental environment was one in which the man was the breadwinner. Period. If he even tried to shift into the role of supplementary support, his inner voice would nag, *Jack, you are the man of the house. You need to get a job. Melissa is beautiful. If she isn't properly cared for, she might leave, she might cheat. Dale just bought a car for Anna. What have you bought for Melissa?*

When Jack's world no longer looked like he thought it must, he had trouble coping and allowed negativity to overtake his thoughts. When he could no longer command the circumstances surrounding him, he felt inadequate, uncertain, no longer "good enough," and this perception of failure threatened his central relationship. Jack's life had been mapped out for him, he'd thought, but his dreams and desires came to a screeching halt, leaving him far more vulnerable than he was comfortable with. All because of an economic recession. Something totally out of his control, outside of himself and his marriage.

One of my professors once said, "It is difficult to see yourself when you are in the picture frame." Jack couldn't see clearly and think objectively about his current situation when he was in the middle of it. But the truth is, we can't control everything in our lives. The stock market can crash, a depression can hit, we can experience an unexpected loss at any time. It's difficult for many of us to come to the realization that we can't control everything in our lives, and this is the inner struggle: get frustrated and flail against new realities when they come upon us or accept and evolve with them.

In Jack's case, he had to find a way to deal with a whole new reality, a different environment than he'd ever considered for himself. To do so—to teach his inner critic to start communicating different, more positive messages to him, messages that reminded him of the temporary nature of his circumstances but the steadfast elements of his values and ethics—he and Melissa had to clearly communicate their needs. When people do not communicate their needs, the negative inner critic will rear its ugly head and override good judgment. This causes unnecessary arguments that have nothing to do with the core problem. Staying focused on the core issue at hand—not all the debris flying around it, urging us to go down futile paths and detouring our better intentions—is the best way to address it.

Resisting Environmental Conflicts: The Parable of the Grasshopper and the Crow

An African proverb says, "A fight among grasshoppers is a joy to the crow." What does that mean? When we fight among ourselves, we become weaker as a team and are vulnerable to outside influences. In this metaphor, the crow represents the enemy outside of the relationship. Unhealthy arguments lead to resentment and distrust and give outside influences an opportunity to attack the relationship.

Outside influences (that, admittedly, often morph into inside influences as well) can include: an extramarital affair, a bad habit, an ongoing addiction, debt, an interfering family member squatting in your home, a highly critical boss. The crow can come in many forms. It likes to feed on insecurity and uncertainty in a relationship. When we make the mistake of treating the symptoms of insecurity and uncertainty with alcohol or other vices to escape stress within the relationship or to escape what's going on inside us, the crow only grows in strength, only has more to prey on. I've seen it time and time again.

Describe in your journal how you let the crow into your personal life. By heeding an inner voice that nudges you to be petty, small, selfish, and defensive, have you created a pattern that's now hurting your relationship? Have you let useless squabbling interrupt domestic peace and harmony? Did you let down your defenses against negative influences instead of fighting for what you know is right and good?

In any relationship—including the one you have with yourself—it's never too late to fortify your walls to keep the crow out. You do this by utilizing effective communication skills, repairing trust, acknowledging your wrongs, putting good energy back into the relationship, and creating a system that is founded on love. The end result is constructing a scarecrow that keeps the crow away, protecting the fabric and sanctity of the relationship.

Influence #3: Communication

Your way of communicating, whatever forms it takes, can have great influence on the way the inner critic influences you. Who do you talk to? Who do you listen to? What kind of thoughts do your own words and the words of others invite into your mind?

There's this story I heard a long time ago. In China, there was a purge against Christians. Among the imprisoned Christians, three believers refused to renounce their faith despite all the torture they were subjected to for years. Finally, the prison warden had had enough. He informed his superior that he would put the three men to death first thing the following morning. His superior asked him not to. Instead, they were transferred to an unknown room, and a record was played repeatedly every minute of every day. The record contained atheistic and anti-Christian proclamations. The three Christians, who didn't renounce their Christian faith after years of torture, did so in less than a year. They renounced—not under duress, but under the power of repetitive communication.

Some people say, "Men are moved by what they see, and women are moved by what they hear." I don't agree. I think both men and women are moved by what they see and hear just in different ways. Ever heard two military buddies talking? Their form of communication is wrapped in their military culture. Their behavior is a direct result of this form of repetitive and familiar communication. The same is true of both men and women.

There are two types of communication: verbal and nonverbal. Verbal communication, also called oral communication, consists of information being passed from one person to another via words. Healthy communication is a two-way street. But communication is not healthy, functional, or complete if one party does not understand what the other is trying to say. This does not mean that ineffective or incomplete communication cannot affect the way someone views themselves, the other person, and the relationship. But it does mean that being clear, concise, and assertive holds power when communicating your feelings and thoughts to another person.

Some people struggle with communicating their feelings because fear dominates their decision to express their needs. They are fearful of what the other person might think of them. They are fearful of losing the trust of the other person. They are fearful because they believe that the person they care for will get angry, offended, or turned off and decide to walk away from them, furthering their fear of abandonment.

Negatively Charged Language

At some point in your life, I'm sure you've met people who only have negative things to tell you. They are unhappy with everything and want you to be unhappy along with them. It's true that misery loves company. When you encounter people who seem like they never have anything positive to say, it's likely attributed to the fact that they are receiving attention from others through the malady of negativity, for it's also true that any attention is better than no attention for some.

Now, *why* these people transmit only negative messages is a different discussion—That's a whole different book! —but somewhere along the way, they picked up the notion that positivity can't be trusted. They're safer in their womb of doom for any number of reasons: highly critical caregivers who modeled to them that care must equate to criticism, an extremely disappointing series of life events, an intense fear of vulnerability that automatically erects a defensive barrier, a broken heart, intense loneliness or isolation, a sense of powerlessness in the world that causes them to invent this form of power to influence others, maybe even a personality disorder, chemical imbalance, or cognitive deficit left untreated. Without going into the specific reasons some people cling to negative language, for our purposes what's important is that such language can become toxic to our souls and can seep into various parts of our lives.

And what should you do when you encounter something toxic? Stay away from it. You do not have to abandon people in need to refuse to engage in meaningless and hurtful exchanges with them. You can set boundaries, and the strong arm of your inner critic can create its own defensive barrier against targeted attacks or even just general negative words that muddy your vision and lead to self-doubt. What you can't do is let the words sink in, leaving permanent scars. Maybe you didn't have control over negative talkers when you were a child— maybe the damage done then still needs to be undone now—but you do have control as an adult, and you can mitigate, if not eradicate, negatively charged language from your daily life.

Negative verbal communication settles into our conscious and subconscious minds and then burrows in deep there. I'm sure you can recall at least one negative comment in your life that will stick with you forever, that you'll never forget, and that will continue to influence you for the rest of your life. That one instance proves the point about the potency of negative communication and why we must try to avoid it at all costs. Take this time to think back in times past to a hurtful event in your life when something was said about you. Write about this instance in your therapy journal and let your emotions and thoughts run free.

Here's the good news: Positive communication settles into our minds too. Positively charged language also has power, authority, lasting impact. That's why therapy, self-help books, affirmations, and meditation are so effective—the human brain can learn to reset and redirect itself; we can turn off the faulty tapes in our head and write new scripts; negativity can be neutralized with positivity.

So how much negativity have you been listening to lately? Note in your journal how much derision, spite, pride, violence, or darkness is entering, or you allow to enter, your world. Negative communication generates negative thought patterns and a negative inner voice. Positive communication generates positive thought patterns and a positive inner voice. It's that straightforward.

Miscommunication in Our Primary Relationships

Most forms of communication are not as clear-cut as negatively charged language, however. Most of our communication occurs with the people who figure most prominently in our everyday lives. Let's take a look at a common type of interaction between two people, and although this example features married couple Derek and Lorinda, the communication concepts can apply to any relationship in your life—with your kids, parents, siblings, friends, or coworkers. We most often communicate—or miscommunicate—with our significant other, though, so I'm sure this exchange will sound familiar:

Lorinda says, "You never spend enough time with me. I feel like I'm alone most of the time. When we do go out occasionally, you seem like you're just so distracted that you're not really there."

Derek says, "I don't know what you want from me, I'm doing the best I can. This house costs money. The kids' school costs money. I have to work as much as I do to provide for the family. I don't think you really appreciate the hard work I put in for the family."

This is a pretty classic case of miscommunication of unmet needs between both parties. Lorinda is feeling alone in the relationship even though Derek is physically present. Derek is feeling like he's not being appreciated for the effort he devotes to taking care of his family. It is important to note that it is not a matter of being right or wrong. This situation has everything to do with the *feelings* of each person.

From Derek, the crow in this instance would latch on to the feeling of unappreciation, and from Lorinda, the crow would exploit feelings of loneliness and neglect. As the couple's negative inner critics begin to speak to them, feelings of uncertainty arise. The crow then summons various additional enemies to unravel the fabric of the relationship—past slights, third parties, substance use, known childhood triggers—to cover up the real pain that is surfacing between the two. All this uncertainty and miscommunication just inflames the already-smoldering insecurity. It's a vicious cycle of not listening to the other person saying what you don't want to hear and tuning in instead to your own mental voice defending your position and telling you why you're right.

When the Crow Wins

Derek and Lorinda are engaging in a destructive form of communication. It's an accusatory form, in which one person puts the blame on the other for a perceived wrong by pointing out what the person isn't doing right. This communication style clearly does not lead to greater intimacy within the relationship; instead, it draws people away from each other and into the dark recesses of old insecurities in their subconscious minds. Without effectively processing problems through positive forms of communication, without being clear, concise, and assertive, it is inevitable that old issues will come back to haunt the relationship. It is inevitable that the crow will circle above, sneeringly laughing at our attempts to squelch the inner mutterings telling us to stubbornly hold fast to our stance. Here's why:

When Lorinda says, "You never spend enough time with me," the accusation just adds more pressure on Derek than he's already feeling from a schedule that's overwhelming him. In response, he becomes more resistant, frustrated, angry, and resentful. So he just retreats from the situation entirely—hurriedly heads out to the gym, then sequesters himself in his man cave with the ball game for the rest of the night once he returns home. From this position in his "foxhole," a sort of psychological warfare commences between the couple.

Next comes punishing significant others through passive-aggressive behaviors, such as silencing and distancing, which Derek engages in now. (It should be noted that males and females are equally guilty of retreat and passive-aggressiveness, it's just that in this particular scenario, Derek happens to be culprit.) Silencing can be unthinkably cruel. It creates a thick, invisible wall or force field that puts a heavy burden on the relationship. By silencing Lorinda, Derek is essentially completely invalidating his wife—purposely ignoring her and not even acknowledging her presence. In the process, he does not see her as a whole person, as a spiritual being, as an equal to him in terms of emotions and power. Held apart from her husband by a force field of his own making, this form of punishment leaves Jane feeling uncomforted, unprotected, alone, and utterly vulnerable.

Lorinda's inner critic then begins reacting as one would expect. She doubts that her husband truly cares about her, she assumes he has no desire to be intimate with her and no longer finds her attractive. He doesn't care about the well-being of their marriage, she tells herself, and he's unforgiving. Her attempts at communication only result in being silenced, creating a feeling of walking on eggshells in her own home, so she decides to stop communicating.

Now there's silence on both sides. This is a code red!

Lorinda's emotional door begins to close—sometimes this happens more quickly than you'd expect. She becomes cold and distant, going about her normal routines of washing the dishes, doing the laundry, and making dinner, but her emotional attachment to Derek is dying. On the outside, they exchange pleasantries after work, they pay the bills, they visit their families. But on the inside, Lorinda has convinced herself that their whole marriage has been a farce and she begins the process of mentally grieving the loss of her relationship, the loss of love. She may even be preparing herself for departure, readying herself to move on. Her mindset has shifted from thoughts of reconciliation to thoughts of flight. Some people don't even see this coming. Derek might just come home one day to find an empty house.

In such an extreme situation? When this kind of dynamic sets a precedent that then repeats itself more frequently over time? When two people stop talking to each other and only talk to themselves until they grow farther and farther apart, becoming strangers to one another? The crow hasn't just been circling—it's eaten the grasshoppers!

Language Shifting

Using the psychological sense of the term, a solution to miscommunication is *language shifting*. Shifting the form and content of human communication helps the speaker and the listener work through issues so they can resolve the problem. The beauty of language shifting is that you don't have to be at odds with someone to employ this strategy. I've already touched on the importance of being clear, concise, honest, and assertive in communicating true feelings. By incorporating these ingredients into your language, you will direct issues that you are having with the listener away from the person and toward the problem. When you stay rooted in the present, authentic in your immediate emotions, and when you don't veer off on irrelevant tangents, objectivity trumps subjectivity, allowing you to properly assess and more accurately weigh the intentions, mindset, thoughts, opinions, and current feelings of the listener. In turn, as a direct result of effective communication with someone you care about, intimacy grows, as does your understanding of yourself, your self-concept, self-confidence, self-respect, and self-esteem. This is the core of language shifting. You can begin with this foundation and then build upon it to make it yours once you have these basic principles down. Let's return to Derek and Lorinda to see these principles in practice.

If Lorinda shifted her language from the accusatory "You never spend enough time with me" to "I feel lonely because your time is taken away by work," it eliminates the pressure on Derek to actually do more, perform more, because the statement isn't blaming him for any wrongdoing, it's merely a simple and honest expression of her feelings. The value of "I feel because" statements isn't a new concept— but it's so pervasive in the therapy world *because it works*. Many of my clients initially feel that this way of communicating is awkward or unnatural. Nevertheless, the very reason so many of them seek therapy is because of the breakdown in their communication style, so it's worth a try, right?

Many people are also uncomfortable connecting to their feelings, let alone expressing them to the other person. Some believe it's a form of weakness to talk so openly about their emotions and expose themselves to others. Some were raised to communicate instead through anger, passive-aggressive behaviors, sarcasm, ignoring, or silence. None of these tactics help resolve the problem, though; on the contrary, they exacerbate conflict to the point of frustrating progress between couples, among families, or in the individual. When you consciously practice the principles of language shifting, however— straightforwardly and honestly sharing a feeling without judgment or condemnation of the other—you will see for yourself how it transforms potentially heated interactions into mutually beneficial ones, which will inspire you to continue working on this style of communication and customizing it for your particular needs and relationships.

For Derek and Lorinda, her language-shifted comment— "I feel lonely because your time is taken away with work"—clearly communicates that the problem is the problem, Derek is not the source of the problem. And the problem is time management, something that is fixable—it's not Derek who needs to be fixed. Together they can work on finding a balance that resolves this issue.

Not only that, but the words Lorinda has chosen to use

communicate to Derek how important he is to her. He hears that she misses him, and this underscores how precious their time together as a couple is. With just one changed statement, blame is taken out of the conversation, growth is promoted, and intimacy in the marriage is reinforced. Moreover, Lorinda has begun to establish assertiveness in her communication, she's building confidence in her stronger voice, and she's learned that her words matter.

In healthy communication, for Derek's part, he would say in reply, "What I am hearing from you is that you feel lonely in our relationship because a lot of my time is devoted to work, and this bothers you." This is another simple technique imparted in therapy that clients sometimes initially scoff at, but again, when they try it, they see that it works. First, Derek is acknowledging Jane's feelings. He is showing her that he's listening and is accurately assessing her experience. Properly repeating back what someone has said to you is such a powerful tool with men in particular because many men are accused of being insensitive. They try to *fix* the situation instead of *understanding* the speaker's feelings. When men explain away a problem or give reasons why this or that happened, it communicates that they do not care about their partner's feelings and only care about being right or justified. The irony about this way of communicating is that the man might be *logically* correct but *emotionally* wrong.

By shifting their communication style, the couple can both get their needs met. Derek feels appreciated, loved and respected by Lorinda. Lorinda feels empowered by taking a healthy step to get more time with her husband. United, they can tackle the problem of time management that will ultimately strengthen their relationship and increase their happiness.

Derek and Lorinda could easily have been carried away on the waves of destructive communication if they just went back and forth blaming each other. We've all been there—you know what that kind of exchange leads to: a cesspool of stagnation, bitterness, and resentment. Blame and grudges are like a cancer: The more they are left untreated, the more they head toward a terminal end. But using "I feel because" statements allows the brain to understand and process the feelings of the other person in arguments or disagreements without getting offended. Practicing this dual style of self-referential speaking and reflective listening will eventually become more fluid. You'll find it easier to communicate with others without repeating the same dead-end conversations and exacerbated problems.

It's worth noting before we leave Derek and Lorinda that it wouldn't sense for him to argue against her feelings of loneliness and neglect by telling her why she shouldn't "feel" that way because those feelings belong to her. She has a right to have them and express them. By coming to an understanding of them through reflective listening instead of trying to explain them away, the intimacy both yearn for in their marriage increases. By incorporating language shifting, the narrative of their marriage will begin to take on more and more of a positive storyline that involves less and less criticism. Eventually, they can look back on the chapters of their lives together and take pride in learning to override ingrained thought patterns that are no longer serving them and instead heed the higher voice of positive communication.

Influence #4: Childhood

Our early years are some of the most important in life. Broadly speaking, childhood can be defined as the period from birth to young adulthood, and although the commencement of adulthood varies across nations, it typically begins in the United States at age eighteen. We've obviously intersected the influence of childhood on the development of our inner critic in the preceding sections— there's no way of talking about relationships, environments, and communication in our lives without considering the origins of all those things from a very young age. But here we'll zero in just a bit on who we are before we even know who we are.

We are born into this world with no choice as to our parents, culture, heritage, religion, nationality. We grow up to the sounds of the languages our parents and siblings speak. From infancy to toddlerhood, we are spoon-fed everything we eat, we're spoken to in words we don't comprehend, we're thrown in the air, cuddled, tickled, and bathed by the hands of strangers we slowly begin to recognize who quickly become the dearest and most precious thing in our lives. Our family.

We start to pick up on conversations and witness events we likely will not remember. Gradually, though, we begin to form attitudes from those conversations and events. We see Father eat, and we register that food is consumed using utensils or fingers. We hear Mother sing, and we're inaugurated into the wonder of melody, tone, rhythm, and rhyme. We see numbers and letters and join them to make meaning out of the union. Through it all, we start to become aware of feelings—joy, pain, failure, terror, jealousy, sadness, silliness, pride, curiosity.

During the school-aged years, choices become available and grow wider as we mature. We might not have chosen our families, addresses, or communities, but we get to choose our friends, the books we want to read, the music we want to download, our favorite foods and color and clothing styles, how much time we spend alone versus with others, what kind of student we want to be, what career we want to pursue. We're limited in our actions in the beginning, yes, but as our brains develop, our cognitive abilities advance to higher levels of thinking. So do our emotional abilities. We can choose to lie, to negotiate, to manipulate, to strive, to succumb, to prevail.

Where am I going with all of this universally understood information? It goes without saying that the formative years hold experiences that directly and unquestionably influence who we will or will not become. No one is immune to this. Happy family or dysfunctional mess. Murderer or the Dalai Lama. Whether you're born in North Dakota or Nairobi. Whether you grow up to be a chemist or a carpenter. We're all exposed to experiences that profoundly and irrefutably shape what and who we will become. Some of the nuances of these experiences lie so deep in our unconscious or subconscious that we cannot grasp the degree to which they sway and steer us, but they're there nevertheless.

So in continuing the discussion of our inner critic, it's important to realize that the influence of childhood isn't just a part of it, it's the breeding ground for it—the nascency of the life span cannot be separated from the nascency of the inner critic. Each and every moment of our lives, over the totality of our existence from the day we were born up to today, we're taking in information: observations, sensations, impressions, you name it. Our bodies, our brains, and our souls are the receptacles of all that data, but it's the inner critic that gives voice to how it's processed and interpreted. Although we cannot access what's lodged in the unconscious, our inner critic has the ability to draw strength from all realms of the brain—the conscious, the subconscious, and the unconscious—and put things into words we can understand. Even if they're not objectively true. Even if they hurt us more than help us. That's why it's so essential to understand the language of your mind.

Simply put, the nature of your childhood is the very essence of your inner critic. Your inner critic can evolve and mature and let go and learn another language just like you can, but you share the same origin story. If you want to advance toward ever-higher levels of enlightenment, you'll have to grow together.

Influence #5: The Internal Factor of the Self

Thus far, all of the factors we've covered have been external. This last influence on our inner critic is far more internal in nature, and yet it's challenging to explain because it's rather abstruse and esoteric. Far more abstract than concrete. Untouchable and almost inexplicable. I'm talking about the part of you that is uniquely yours and yours alone—the part that came attached to your spirit or your soul or whatever word you prefer to use to talk about your divine individuality as a human being unlike any other human being who ever has or will ever live.

This is the part of you that wasn't coded, but instead came hard-wired. It is independent of your genetic makeup. It would be the same regardless of environment, no matter the people you have relationships with and the things they say and do to you. It was there from birth and started revealing itself in childhood, but it wasn't planted there and you never outgrow it.

For lack of a better term, I'm going to call this ineffable quality your personality. But try to go beyond the dictionary definition of what you've always understood the word to mean and see it as both a composite of and also greater than the words contained within it: your very "person," that's unequivocally "personal"—your very own "it"-ness. I know that many will argue that some of our inborn traits are inherited, are learned, are environmentally dependent. But I truly believe that there's a kernel of singularity in each of us that neither science nor psychology nor nurturing can explain.

Annabel just came out of the womb bold—she was an active kicker inside, her mother recalls, and she's stayed that way all her life, even coming from a small town that offered little in the way of adventure or opportunity, even though she had no particular aptitude for many of the interests she pursued, even though she holds a regular nine-to-five job that masks the invincible fierceness underneath that defines her to herself. Her brother, Jeremy, was timid from birth—not because Annabel intimidated or bullied him, not because a childhood experience traumatized him—he's just innately quiet and shy and meek. Same household, same upbringing, same parenting, and same community, but the two are polar opposites. Raymond feels most alive when white water rafting; Frieda is at her absolute happiest when gardening. Christine connects with her authentic self when she's out in nature, smelling the moss and hearing a bubbling brook; Lashaun says he's "home" when poring over black holes—they mesmerize him, captivate him at a soul level, bring meaning to his existence. No reason for these innate natures, they just *are*.

I'm thinking of another woman I know, Patty, whose mother left a lot to be desired. Patty was not encouraged, emotionally nourished, complimented, or well guided in her young life. In fact, she was rebuked for being chubby, ignored and neglected for most of childhood, and labeled "stupid" in school for what would later reveal itself as dyslexia. And yet Patty told me, "I always knew I was special. I always knew I had greatness in me. I never doubted it for a second and no one could convince me otherwise. When I picked up a paintbrush, I discovered that would be the vehicle to show my greatness, but even if I hadn't been a talented artist, I would have found my greatness elsewhere. The world can be tough. I'm tougher. Inside. It's what makes me me. The inner knowing I've always had." I have a feeling Mozart would agree that his genius didn't stem from his ancestors, his surroundings, his friendships, or his experiences either.

The internal factor of the self influences our actions and decisions, and those actions and decisions result in the experiences and information that are stored in our conscious and subconscious mind. And as we've already learned, the voice of the inner critic draws from this wellspring when it speaks to us. There's no mathematical formula set out that can determine to what percentage and in what proportion each factor influences the inner critic, but let's just say selfhood carries clout!

We'll spend some more time talking about the internal factor of the self in later chapters. Here, I just want you to take in that your unique fingerprint of selfhood is yet another element that flavors the voice and motivations of the inner critic inside you. I've already introduced you to my own personal sense of self, which you know greatly values my African heritage. In keeping with this affinity, I'll conclude this discussion with some food for thought by listing various self-based concepts that figure prominently in African philosophy:

- Self-concept: how we define ourselves (*Swahili*-Jitambue "To know thyself").
- Self-confidence: the belief in our definition of ourselves (*Swahili*- Kujiamini- "To believe in one's self").

- Self-esteem: the umbrella that draws energy from the two preceding underlying concepts, coupled with our abilities (*Swahili*-Kujithamini "To draw power from self-esteem")
- The collective self: how we are empowered by positive people in the greater community, not just individually (*Swahili*-Nguvu ya umoja- The power of togetherness)

Summary

This chapter aimed to lay the groundwork for what is to follow by delineating the multiple sources of the inner critic's voice. Before you can learn to work with that voice and put it to good, better, positive use for you in your everyday relationships and actions, it's essential to understand what you're up against: just how many factors have gone into configuring, energizing, and sustaining that voice over your lifetime. But like any entity, the inner critic is more than just the sum of its parts—it can be divided into components, but it exists as a whole unto itself.

Similarly, African tribes view the family as a collective whole. In traditional life, the individual does not and could not exist alone. Of course there is mother, father, son, daughter, but the family unit supersedes any individual member, and the larger tribe supersedes any individual family. "It takes a village to raise a child" is a saying that became popular in the United States during a particular political climate, but it's actually an age-old African proverb that signifies that there's no division among even extended family in the community. The success of the child is dependent on the family and the involvement of the community. What is your larger community? What supports do you have outside of your immediate household? Lets take some time to write them down in your journal.

All of this speaks to the many and diverse elements that contribute to the modern-day therapeutic landscape. Within recovery models and strength- and evidence-based practices, counselors are beginning to recognize the importance of culture in the therapeutic process. Therapists are also seeing the value of indigenous spiritual and healing practices in therapy sessions. Approaches to family systems play a part in these evolving discoveries.

In the Western world, counseling, interventions, medications, and guidance from clergy members and mentors are some of the ways families and people have been helped in difficult times. In Africa, libations, healing ceremonies, and cleansing rituals have helped families through difficult times. These practices can serve a vital role in effective therapy—a spiritual component can add untold value. Just as awareness of the culture of my people helped me transcend some of my own problems, awareness of your own family's culture—along with the other factors discussed in this chapter—can connect you to a story that is greater than your own and that can help you move past the pitfalls that keep tripping you up.

The inner critic will have you believe that your struggles will never end—for acceptance, for inclusion, for understanding, for inner peace. That's simply not true—it's a delusion. If the inner critic is powerful enough to convince you of your limitations, mightn't it be powerful enough to convince you that you can overcome them? I return to the beginning: Your story is much larger than what the inner critic wants you to believe. When you are aware and awake to the world around you and your successes in it, you reclaim your role as the author of your own story. So what voice in your head do you want to listen to: the limiting one, the empowering one, or the neutral one? We turn now to the nature of each and how you can channel them to your advantage.

CHAPTER 4

The Positive Voice, the Negative Voice, and the Voice of Objectivity

As a man thinketh in his heart, so is he.

—Proverbs 23:7

On May 25, 1961, President John F. Kennedy delivered a speech to both houses of Congress. He stated that the United States should set a goal of "landing of a man on the moon and returning him safely" by the end of the decade. Nearly nine years after, NASA blasted off *Apollo 11*.

Neil Armstrong, Edwin "Buzz" Aldrin, and Michael Collins were the astronauts on *Apollo 11*. Four days after takeoff, on July 20, 1969, they landed the lunar module *Eagle*, and Neil Armstrong became the first man to set foot on the moon. He and Buzz Aldrin walked around on the moon, conducted experiments, and picked up bits of moon rocks and dirt. Michael Collins stayed in orbit around the moon and conducted experiments. Neil and Buzz left a sign on the moon that reads HERE MEN FROM THE PLANET EARTH FIRST SET FOOT UPON THE MOON JULY 1969, A.D. WE CAME IN PEACE FOR ALL MANKIND.

All of it stemmed from JFK's declaration to Congress. Words hold power. Words can make things happen. Words—the language of humankind—steer both accomplishments and setbacks, goals and glitches, our sense of self and our sense of the world. And they start inside. Well before Kennedy ever delivered those lines, he would have pondered long and hard about the meaning of them, the commitment they bounded him to, the way they would impact countless lives. His internal critic would have warned him, advised him, coached him, worried him. Ultimately, the strong voice of victory would win the debate over the voice of trepidation and doubt, and his internal musings would become a reality out loud.

Everything in life has sources, and sources are rooted internally before they're expressed externally. When we're talking about the voice of the inner critic, its sources are located in the past and the present, and the level and consistency of that voice—how loudly we hear it and how negatively charged, positively charged, or not charged at all it is—depend in kind on the negativing, positivity, or neutrality of its sources.

The Positive Voice

As we know, the inner critic can reveal itself in different garbs at different times in different circumstances. The positive aspect of the inner critic can be thought of as the good voice, the voice of the angel on your shoulder, your own personal cheerleader, even your own best friend. It is the voice of quiet reproach that cautions us when we are tempted to do something wrong. It is the voice that reassures us when we fear we might collapse or fail. When we are feeling most unfit, it tells us that we are capable and competent. It communicates closely with our inbred moral code and conscience.

In *The Autobiography of Malcolm X*, Malcolm wrote about his experience growing up in foster care. His father was a Baptist preacher who fought against white oppression and for freedom of the Negro, and he was killed by Klansmen in the rural South. His sermons espoused the beliefs of Marcus Garvey in the early 1900s. After his father's murder, Malcolm's mother did the best she could to raise ten children on her own, but her struggles led to her children being taken away by social services, where Malcolm was separated from his brothers and sisters. His mother would eventually succumb to significant mental health issues and was placed in a mental health ward after losing her children. Despite all this hardship, Malcolm was head of his class and was a proficient debater among his peers. When asked by a teacher what he would like to be, he said he wanted to be a lawyer. His teacher replied, "A lawyer is no job for a nigger. You should be a carpenter like Jesus."

These experiences of Malcolm's youth shaped his sociopolitical beliefs. His own moral code was learned from his father and mother and infused with such values as self-respect, diligence, and hard work. His intelligence and eloquence became his trademarks in his later years and helped him convey meaningful messages to his listeners, even though much of those messages was fueled with anger and hurt from his past and his present.

Before being assassinated by the same people he worked side by side with in the Nation of Islam, Malcolm would take that iconic photo with Dr. Martin Luther King Jr., smiling and shaking hands. He would renounce the idea of separatism between white and Black after his pilgrimage to Mecca. He experienced white brothers who ate from the same plate as him and drank from the same cup, showing no partiality or prejudice. He returned to America with a new sense of hope for both White and Black people in the struggle for equality.

The positive inner critic derives from things, places, and experiences that motivate, elevate, teach, correct, and caution us. In Malcom's case, as with many other Black Americans, it derived from his experiences with people who could not see him as being equal.

His journey would lead him to see the truth of good and evil in a world not based on color, gender, or nationality. This truth would be evident in his relations with the nonviolent white Muslims he met and with some of the envy-driven Black Islamic members of his religious faction under Elijah Muhammed. This irony would eventually come full circle and change his course of thinking and outlook on human behavior. Tragically, he did not live long enough to fully appreciate the beauty of human connectiveness, despite differences in skin color.

No one did more to further the vision of that connectiveness than Dr. King himself, through his activism and his legendary speeches— all emanating from his positive inner voice—most notably his "I Have a Dream" speech, delivered on August 28, 1963, at the Lincoln Memorial in Washington, DC. In that immortal speech, he put into words his dream of a day when we would no longer be judged by the color of our skin, but by the content of our character. He could have given up his cause before this March on Washington. After multiple arrests and attempts on his life, after being attacked by police dogs and sprayed by fire hoses, he could have heeded the negative inner critic telling him that the barriers were insurmountable, that his dream for equality would never come to pass. But his inner strength and self-determination prevailed up to the end, even as he foreshadowed his own demise in his last speech on April 3, 1968, at Mason Temple: "I've been to the mountaintop. ... And I've looked over. And I've seen the promised land. I may not get there with you ... but we, as a people, will get to the promised land!"

The next day, on April 4, 1968, Dr. Martin Luther King Jr. was assassinated. At six o'clock p.m., when King was standing on the balcony of the Lorraine Motel in Memphis, Tennessee, James Earl Ray fired the fatal shot from his rifle.

More than forty years later, on January 20, 2009, we saw the inauguration of the first African American president of the United States of America. I remember the tears of joy that flowed down my cheeks when I thought about all the people before him who had the faith to believe, to fight, and to die for that moment to be possible.

He ran on a platform of "hope" and "change," and you can bet that his later campaign of "Yes, we can" also referred to the passion and perseverance inside him: *Yes, I can.*

Our words have power! The words inside our minds and the words that come out as a result. These historic figures, and many others, exemplify what it means to be guided by your positive inner critic, to let that aspect rise to the fore above all others—against the grain, against all odds, and at any cost.

Believing What You See and Hear

Belief in something arises from observed experiences. Belief can arise in other ways, sure—religious faith, for example, can firmly exist without evidence, scientific data, or firsthand knowledge—but believing in something most often comes from experiencing something yourself. If you read a book or watched a news story about a man who survived at sea for three days after a shipwreck, you'd find cause to believe in survival, in the will to live overcoming the capitulation to perish. If you saw your mother avoid eviction by working three jobs to keep a roof over your head, you'd believe that hard work, sacrifice, and sheer persistence can bring about desired results. And when you were struggling mightily with geometry, if your favorite math teacher told you, "If you keep studying, if you keep at it, you will not only master this subject, but you will learn to master anything you set your mind to," you'd start to believe that she might be right. If she believed in you, there's something to believe in, right?

The things we see and the words we hear in our youth follow us onward, to college and beyond, influencing our decisions at every turn. What is told to us and what we take in with our own senses are the raw material from which the inner voice is shaped. Thereafter, it's the words of the inner voice that will urge you to go on when you yourself face a life-or-death decision ... it's the inner voice transformed into outward behavior that will talk you into staying in the dorm to study for the exam instead of going out partying with your friends. When you think about quitting a job at twenty-seven years old because you're clashing with your boss, it's your mother's modeled behavior that will whisper to your inner voice that you shouldn't quit until you have a new job, that you have bills to pay, responsibilities to meet. You saw it, you learned it, it became incorporated into the inner critic's vocabulary.

And what we see and hear doesn't even need to be addressed directly to us—President Kennedy's declaration to make it to the moon is an example of that: It planted the seeds of belief in every listener. Similarly, when he said, "Ask not what your country can do for you, ask what you can do for your country," an entire nation thought, *Yeah, what* can *I do to make things better?* An entire nation believed each citizen had something to contribute, had an obligation to take an active part in society; each individual had the agency to make a difference. When seeds like these are planted in hearts and minds, they need only be properly nurtured and watered to one day grow into positive mental trees that will bear bountiful fruit.

In his book *Gifted Hands*, Dr. Ben Carson tells his fascinating story of growing up on an inner-city block, in a broken home, and how he transformed himself from a "dummy who couldn't retain much" into one of the leading neurosurgeons in the United States, conducting groundbreaking surgeries and thousands of successful operations. In this motivating book that was later turned into a film, Carson writes extensively about the influential people in his life, like his mother, his English teacher, the director of his ROTC band, Mr. Doakes, and his biology teacher, Mr. Frank McCotter. Each played a pivotal role in helping him become what he could only imagine for himself. Mr. Doakes said, "Carson, you have to put academics first." He did. He heard those words and he heeded them. He believed in them. Then he believed in himself.

Choosing to believe in yourself, in something greater for yourself, and in something greater than yourself is the quickest route to positive life and career results. Yes, thoughts and words must be coupled with actions to bring about the outcomes you want, but those actions start with words and thoughts. People sometimes resist this notion. They tell me no one ever believed in them, or their uncle called them a loser, or their father hammered into their head that they'd never amount to anything. When facing difficulties, their inner critic steps in with what it's been programmed to hear, programmed to say. If you fail, then you'll only be proving your father right. If you drop out of school, your teachers will have been right. If you give up on a marriage that others said wasn't right for you, then they will have known better than you do.

But you don't have to surrender to that negative programming! You can look around you and find plenty to believe in that helps you rather than hinders you, that propels you rather than holds you back. You can try anyway, you can refuse to quit, you can stay in the fight. If you pay attention to the good news around you too—to the positive words and actions that you *know* matter more—then you can become those positive words and actions yourself, you can embody positivity from the inside out.

The Negative Voice

"Holocaust," to me, is the most horrific word in the English language. The word itself dates back much further than the mid-1940s, of course, and applies to any mass slaughter or extensive loss of life to any people anywhere; but I'm talking about the capitalized version: when the Nazi regime purposefully and intentionally murdered more than six million people—most of them European Jews, but also other marginalized groups such as Gypsies and homosexuals—throughout the course of World War II. That deplorable number doesn't even include all the men, women, and children who died during the war— fighting in armies, starving in freezing streets, bombed in cities, buried under rubble, shot out of the sky and drowned in downed boats, succumbing to illness and infections in makeshift hospital beds, executed for trying to aid the persecuted.

And it all started with one man's internal conceptualization of how the world should be—an internal voice that told him why he'd struggled, why his countrymen had struggled, what to do about it, and, most of all, who was to blame for it.

He believed he was a born leader—and not just any leader, the supreme leader. He believed in world domination by one central power. He was anti-Semitic, anti-Communist, anti-democratic and pro-authoritarianism, pro-expansionism, pro-totalitarianism. He categorized people based on their physical attributes, deeming Aryans superior. He believed Germany had been cruelly betrayed and mistreated on the world stage in the aftermath of World War I. He believed in absolute obedience to superiors. He engaged in an extreme form of scapegoating—the most extreme we've ever seen and hopefully will ever see. Don't take my word for it. Read *Mein Kampf*—it's all there, all the stuff we've been talking about that fuels and drives the inner critic: his childhood home, his influences in school, the birth and evolution of his thought processes and belief system that formed the foundation of Nazism.

Yes, Adolf Hitler's deep-seated and depraved vision of reality caused the most heinous event to ravage the globe in modern history. Millions upon millions of lives cut brutally short, people incinerated alive, towns decimated, monuments obliterated, desperate emigrations and immigrations, families shattered for generations, countries becoming friends or enemies virtually overnight, boundary lines redrawn for decades, treaties signed, laws changed, tribunal trials held, the first atomic bomb to ever be dropped on the planet ... all because of ONE MAN'S VOICE. Inside his own mind, he was victimized, justified, and *right*. And someone was going to have to pay for it. He would manifest his perverted internal ramblings as perverted external actions—and the world would never be the same because of it.

Hitler's voice may have spawned evil, but my, did it have power!

It was strong, passionate, dedicated, and authentic. It was resolute, unrelenting, and potent. It admitted no wrong, allowed no doubt, granted no leniency, and remained steadfast under any kind of pressure.

Hitler's voice was so compelling, in fact, that once he'd convinced himself that his belief system was wholly justified, he convinced others, too. His countrymen so wanted something to believe in, to lift them, to unite them in moral outrage that they blindly accepted his righteousness and superiority too. Not all Germans happily and voluntarily fell in line, of course—there were many resisters and deserters and dissenters who saved as many lives as they could ... but not enough. Not nearly enough. Basically all of Germany marched to Hitler's orders, whether out of loyalty, devotion, national pride, jealousy, rage, fear, or coercion. I don't mean to invalidate a human being's basic instinct to do whatever it takes to survive, but if enough opposing voices had risen up early on, then the masses mightn't have been so broadly silenced later. And it wasn't just people who were swayed by Hitler's seductive voice, his sadistic vision. Other countries got on board also. Mussolini's Italy and Hirohito's Japan. Hungary, Romania, Bulgaria.

All in all, there were 75 million casualties of a worldwide war— the deadliest event in world history—essentially orchestrated by one man's cognitive processing. *That's* how powerful the mind can be. It can wreak devastation and despair. It can create delusions of grandeur or of worthlessness. It can shape a nation. Define lives. Change destiny.

What to make of all this? What do we do with knowledge of the negative critical voice that grows inside some people out of doubt, fear, selfishness, greed? Well, for every point there is a counterpoint, for every sinner a saint, for every pain a pleasure, for every tragedy a triumph. I believe that's the way human existence works: We're never stuck with just one option. I choose to believe that there's a balance to the universe so that things will eventually right themselves, fairness will ultimately prevail.

Adolf Hitler is an extreme example of how the negatively charged inner critic can have dire consequences—he personifies evil, despair, darkness. To offset such a presence, mightn't there be an extreme example in the other direction—a positively charged inner critic fed by goodness, hope, light? Perhaps you've heard of Viktor Frankl? If Hitler represents the very worst a human being can think and act and do when faced with external circumstances he wants to change, here's the story of another man who faced the very worst situation you could possibly imagine and found a way to direct his cognitions in a positive direction instead.

Dr. Viktor Frankl was a Jewish psychiatrist in Austria who was hauled off with his family to a concentration camp in 1942 by German soldiers. Theresienstadt, where his father perished, would be only the first of four camps in which Frankl was imprisoned until 1946. His wife died at one; his mother and brother died at another, the infamous Auschwitz.

During his years-long confinement under the most atrocious conditions, Frankl witnessed so much struggle and strife, so much loss and desolation, truly inconceivable horrors. Already highly trained in suicide prevention and depression, Frankl helped his fellow captives (and surely also himself) survive the ordeal by guiding them to concentrate on positive memories, recollections, thoughts. (Ah, the power of our thoughts again and what they lead us to do!) Frankl believed that even amid dehumanizing and devastating experiences, life had meaning and suffering had a purpose. During the most torturous physical circumstances, one could escape through spiritual means to a state and a place unreachable by external forces.

The tangible result of Frankl's philosophies took the form of a book published in 1946, upon his release. *Man's Search for Meaning*, considered one of the most influential and inspiring books of all time, presents his personal perspective on living through such an inhumane experience, but it also speaks universally to victims of trauma anywhere. The Good Therapy website (goodtherapy.org/famous-psychologists/viktor-frankl.htm) aptly summarizes his intent:

Frankl argues that finding meaning in everyday moments can enable trauma survivors to avoid the bitterness and apathy that are so often the results of torture, imprisonment, and prolonged trauma. He encourages trauma sufferers to think of people they would not want to disappoint, such as dead or distant family members, and to reflect on how they would like to be perceived by these loved ones. Frankl believes meaning can be found through creativity and work, human interaction and experience, and the manner in which we respond to inevitable suffering.

It has been years since I read the book, but I can still visualize Frankl's descriptions of his experiences. His writing style is so vivid that I can still see the muddy coldness of the snow; the frail, sticklike people in black and gray stripes who were emaciated through malnutrition; the mountains of human corpses; the silhouettes of the leafless, gnarled, twisted trees; the vast mass graves beyond the smoke-filled gas chambers; and the coldness in the steel blue eyes of the Nazi soldiers as they followed the orders of the Führer.

The image that stands out to me the most was when Viktor was walking on a cold winter morning. He described his feet being numb from the snow beneath them. He said that he felt like he was going to faint from hunger after being fed only a single potato in the watery soup that morning. As Viktor was walking to his work detail, a little yellow-breasted bird flew over the barbed-wire fence surrounding the camp. The bird landed on the wire that was closest to him, and for a moment, he stared into the eyes of the bird. He felt paralyzed, overcome with emotion. It seemed like the universe had stopped turning. Viktor was transported to a place with no awareness of the cruelty of war, away from the perils of the day. He was in a different time, too—somewhere in the distant future when he would once again taste the sweetness of freedom.

I could see him envisioning himself in his former life. He would be practicing his craft as a psychiatrist, eating and breaking bread with his family and friends, and enjoying the warm embrace of his wife. In the bird's eyes, he saw his future. The bird passed along a message of hope that revealed Viktor's purpose in life. No German solider could touch it. There would be no tanks. No more guns. No more loss of control. There would be no more smell or taste of death all around him, all day, every day. The little bird drew him to a place of transcendence. There, the negative inner critic had no power. There, he could hear only the voice of the positive inner critic. Then, in the here and now, the bird flew off from the fence, over the stone barriers, past the guards, over the German tanks, and into the smoke-filled, pale gray sky.

What Viktor Frankl was describing, I believe, is the spark of hope available to and within anyone, even when they're going through unimaginable pain. If hope could sparkle in him in the middle of a seemingly endless war, in the middle of winter in a death camp, it can sparkle in anyone. Think of a time when you felt depleted of all hope. Think of the lowest of low points in your life, when you couldn't see how in the world you were going to make it out of the situation you were in. When you believed that tomorrow would never come—or when you didn't even want it to. And yet you're still here, reading this book right now. You survived! You made it through! The negative did *not* vanquish the positive. What was your yellow bird? What allowed you to at least glimpse a different reality than the one you felt stuck in then?

The gift of hope is sometimes right in front of our eyes. Oftentimes, we overlook it because we are so engulfed in the stress of the situation. My yellow bird was my mother, my grandmother, and my church mothers. You have a yellow bird too. Look for it when you need it. Do not allow the negative inner critic to conquer the positive inner critic by blinding you to the gift that is always right in front of you. If you were meant to be crushed by your circumstances, you'd be lying facedown in the dirt, utterly defeated; if it was your time to die, you'd be dead. You are greater and stronger than anything that temporarily imprisons you in what feels like a lifelong jail of torment. There is hope—there is always hope! Even in the most extreme of circumstances. And even when under the influence of the four primary traits of the negative voice: self-doubt, fear, unappreciation of self, and selfishness.

Self-Doubt

Even knowing what Frankl knew, even believing in a brighter day somewhere over the rainbow, so many of us allow the negative voice to dominate our daily lives, don't we? That's because the negative voice has various facets to its constitution, and one of those predominant facets is self-doubt. It's a component of the negative voice that makes itself heard in myriad circumstances. When you step into unknown territory, the voice begins to speak. When you're about to start a new job, anxiety can trump anticipation. When you enter into a new relationship, the voice of caution and reluctance often overpowers excitement and trust. If self-doubt pervades even these opportune happenings, imagine the damage it can do elsewhere. When you fail in one particular endeavor, you can bet self-doubt will rear its ugly head the next time you attempt a different endeavor. And if you've experienced a traumatic incident like a life-changing accident, self-doubt has the ability to follow you around like a blanket of helplessness.

Whatever the source of the self-doubt, wherever it derives its strength, it is a negative in life that can hurt a person's chances at success and happiness. People who constantly doubt themselves find it hard to achieve their goals, let alone reach great heights. When a man plagued by self-doubt sees a girl he's attracted to, he immediately assumes she wouldn't like someone like him. So he never asks her out, never even talks to her. When he thinks about a promotion at work, he thinks every other possible candidate must be better for the job than he is. He feels unworthy of happiness and goodness, unworthy of love, joy, wealth, and success.

People who suffer from self-doubt rarely venture outside their comfort zones. They maintain the status quo. They do not challenge themselves to become more. They refrain from voicing their opinions lest they be criticized. They take whatever life hands them because it is comfortable to do so, it gives them the illusion of safety. Every step is carefully planned not to offend anyone. They are great at being average. They do not dare to dream.

Although self-doubt lies deep within the voice of negativity, not everyone heeds its call. High achievers believe in themselves a lot. They fail sometimes, sure, but they rise up over and over again until they get it right. They know self-doubt exists, they just choose not to accept it. Low achievers, however, accept the idea of being a low achiever, so they often don't even bother trying. Because they shy away from pushing limits, they don't learn how to move beyond them and improve. The end result? Their lives are a constant struggle of tumbling over and over within this same cycle of doubt.

Now, you don't have to be a "high" or "low" anything to encounter self-doubt—anyone and everyone will face it at some point in life. It's the level and consistency of it that vary. When it's high and intense, it'll thwart your every move. When it's mild and sporadic, it might only stall you for the short term. For writers, for example, when writer's block sets in, they can see it as only a temporary obstacle capable of bypassing sometime in the near future, or it can grow into a huge boulder that rolls over their belief in themselves as capable and worthy of writing anything that matters. For fighters, the moment they enter the ring with doubts about their ability to win is the moment when they give their opponent a much greater chance to win.

Thoughts on self-doubt for your journal: What are some of your self-doubts? Are they keeping you from accomplishing your dreams? How much or how little? What does the negative inner critic tell you that keeps you doubting over believing?

Fear

We are greatly motivated, often even controlled, by our emotions. Love, hate, lust, affection, envy, and anger—these are just some of the emotions that dictate our actions and words. These emotions have intrinsic value in our lives and sometimes sustain our existence. At every point in life, we are pushed, pulled, encouraged, discouraged, inhibited, and inhabited by one emotion or another.

Fear is one of the most powerful emotions, and as such, it's another primary facet of the voice of the negative critic. A wise man once said, "To make a person do something, instill fear in his heart." Because fear is more of an inhibiting emotion, its voice is most often cautionary. From an evolutionary perspective, fear has served us well. It's caused us to run from wild animals, to protect our young, to find shelter from the storm, and to flee when danger is imminent. I do not fear heights, but I fear jumping from a six-story building—for good reason!

So I'm not talking about the cautionary fear here, the necessary kind. I'm talking about the destructive fear that lives within the inner critic and completely immobilizes us in the face of anything that has the appearance of being tougher than what we think we can handle. They say the fear of failure often leads to failure. Well, overconfidence without proper preparation can sometimes lead to defeat as well, but even the greatest level of preparation, if riddled with fear, will absolutely lead to defeat.

There is a voice that speaks in our hearts and minds—the voice we're becoming more familiar with page after page. When that voice lists all the reasons why you cannot win, it's coming from a mix of fear and doubt. And sometimes it's justified. Think about the Jews who actually survived the Holocaust after World War II. To say that the world now felt like a very unsafe place for them is an understatement. The thought of going back "home," even after the world penalized Germany and stolen property was returned to them, was practically unthinkable. Home was now a place of persecution and gruesome death. The fear must have been paralyzing.

In truth, they had every right to be afraid. The scars were deep, the wounds might never heal, they might recover but never fully be restored. In time, a new home was found for Jews, a place where they'd always belong, where they'd regain their dignity, their equality, their self-respect. A great new state was born. But I doubt the fear will ever entirely go away. Can you blame Holocaust survivors and their children, grandchildren, and great-grandchildren if they think things like, *You can't trust people. The world is a dangerous place. I won't be able to reach my potential. There's no use trying to thrive in a world that doesn't want me to. My life can be taken from me at any moment.* Fear is a part of life, yes, and it figures more prominently in some than in others, for various reasons.

But unchecked fear leads to weakness. It poisons the soul and kills the actions of mind and body. There can be only little progress where fear reigns. It's said that the first rule of winning a fight is to control the breathing and the sight. Why? When the average man is confronted, his fight-or-flight instincts are activated by fear from the spinal cord through the sympathetic nervous system. To control breaths is to let the fear out and to see things as they are. This is a mindfulness technique (which we'll talk about later) that keeps fear in check and courage at the ready. For the voice of fear is a voice that underestimates the self and overestimates the difficulties or odds stacked against the self.

I had the pleasure of meeting the Hall of Fame heavyweight boxing champion Iron Mike Tyson in Las Vegas. I was inspired by him as a kid, and I remember feeling like he was one of the greatest athletes of our time next to Michael Jordan. Studying under his trainer Cus D'Amato as a twenty-year-old, he took the heavyweight championship in 1986 from thirty-five-year-old Trevor Berbick in five minutes thirty-five seconds. He became the youngest heavyweight champion in boxing history.

In an interview, Tyson explained how he knew he had won the boxing match before the fight even began. He said that the moment he saw his opponent break eye contact with him, when the referee was giving them instructions in the middle of the ring, he knew he had him!

Many times, we are faced with odds that seem more difficult or challenging than what we think we can manage. In these times, if our confidence falls prey to our fear, we are defeated before the fight even begins. We second-guess our ability to emerge victorious because we are overwhelmed by trepidation and intimidation. The war that we fight is often more psychological than physical. The winning of the battle begins in the mind. So we have to first imagine the battle already being won in our favor. The second step is to trust our abilities and talents. Third, we have to practice and hone our skills. Fourth, we need to be prepared to sacrifice to overcome the mental fears holding us back. It takes sacrifice to wake up at dawn to get the job done, to save up the money we need to accomplish a goal, to climb the ladder to success, happiness, and fulfillment. You have to work through the pain and have the discipline to encourage yourself when no one else is around. This is the making of a true champion!

Unappreciation of Self

Here is another poison that eats away at the soul. If you find that you constantly compare yourself to your neighbor or consistently think very little of yourself, you might be a victim of self-unappreciation.

This particular injection of the negative voice receives its potency from a repulsion toward the self. This lack of self-regard leads your mind to loop through old scripts: Whatever you do is never good enough. You cannot sing well; you cannot write or read well; you cannot paint or dance well. Your achievements are nothing compared to Deshawn's; you didn't go to an ivy league college like Sheila did; your house isn't as big as the Wilsons'; you can't afford to take a trip with your spouse to celebrate your fifteenth wedding anniversary like Timothy and Samantha did. Therefore, you are nothing. You're worthless. You're a loser.

This aspect of the negative voice haunts a lot of people. It feels like we're in a constant struggle to be better than somebody else. We secretly wish we were in someone else's shoes because of the job they have or the car they drive or the loving mother they have or their beautiful hair. It's like there's a measure of success that must be followed or else we're a complete failure. This kind of thinking is an infection that can fester into a disease.

Self-repulsion can be caused by a number of things: a string of failures, a series of wrong decisions, exposure to people who never have good things to say about you, the wrong friends, or negative family members in your personal space. Self-unappreciation can be traced back to society. When we live in a world where everything is measured by what can be seen, what's on the outside, people tend to value their neighbors more than they value themselves. Social media is good at perpetuating the delusion of self. Their life looks better, so it must be better. Teddy is jealous of James because James has such a wonderful law career, and James secretly wishes he could be like Teddy, with his wonderful wife and children. It's not bad to yearn for a good career or a good marriage, but it's unhealthy and unfruitful when we yearn for things we don't have only because somebody else has them. If we let the voice of unappreciation lead our everyday lives, we will begin to follow other people's dreams instead of our own.

To appreciate yourself is to objectively assess your life, acknowledge your achievements and strengths, admit your mistakes and weaknesses, understand where you are going, and learn from the assessment. For example, an alcoholic must admit that it is up to him to change. He must understand that alcohol has the ability to ruin his attempts at a good life, yet he must not understate his good qualities or underestimate his autonomy to govern his own life. Maybe he's a talented cook who can put that aptitude to work for him. Maybe he's great with kids or animals or home improvements. He might have a heart of gold or exceptional empathy or a great sense of humor. Just because he has a problem with alcohol that he's going to have to deal with, that doesn't mean he doesn't have a promising future ahead and a present that he can grab the reins of now. He can appreciate what he does have and work toward what he wants.

Realistic self-assessment and self-appreciation opens our eyes to our deficits, abilities, and obstacles so that we can chart reasonable and timed strategies to remedy the weaknesses, solidifying the strong areas, navigate the obstacles, and achieve the level of greatness waiting inside all of us.

Selfishness

If you ask me, one of the issues of our society at large is greed and the illusion of happiness. Some of my most interesting clients have been the ones that wanted help with their spending habits. We want everything, we want it now—and then we want more. It seems like it's never enough, nothing is ever good enough. This one wants a prettier wife, that one wants a more luxurious car, the other one wants to replace their six-figure income with seven figures. The 50-inch TV is no longer big enough—time for a 65-incher; the smartphone in hand has to be replaced with the very latest model in the store. Even when we get what we want, there's no end to the coveting, because satisfaction quickly turns to dissatisfaction the moment there's something "even better" to desire.

As a result, American society is largely driven by debt. Payment by plastic. Mortgages people can't afford. Debt that never seems to make it past the interest into the principal. Loans that go unpaid in lieu of designer bags and shoes. And it's not just people who mismanage their resources and misdirect their wants. Companies and financial institutions get greedy too and make very unwise, self-serving decisions. But hey, why do otherwise when you're just going to get bailed out anyway? When fired CEOs get $15 million buyouts? Why do the right thing when the wrong thing isn't penalized? When the very institutions that define the U.S. economy behave recklessly and irresponsibly, why shouldn't our citizenry as well?

As I said before, it's good to want more in life, to want more out of life. Ambition is one of our greatest attributes as human beings; and we'd never move forward if we weren't already looking around the bend to what comes next, to beyond what we already have and already are. All inventions and discoveries, after all, grow out of a yearning for more or to be better.

So wherein lies the problem? When does ambition turn into selfishness? My answer to that is: when our ambitions propel us to get what we want *by any means*. Advancements can have noble causes, but at what price? Finding medical cures at the cost of human life. Manufacturing wonderfully convenient and affordable products, in sweatshops manned with child labor. Stunning diamonds produced by spilled blood in countries like Sierra Leone. Some things simply are not worth the cost—we'll have to get them a different way, a better way.

In *Gifted Hands*, Ben Carson admitted to almost hitting his mother with a hammer in his youth because he wanted "cool clothes." It's understandable that a young man his age wanted to wear what was trendy and fashionable, but this desire was born out of nothing more than wanting to impress his peers, and he was willing to go any lengths to achieve this purely selfish desire. His mother simply couldn't afford what he asked. But he wouldn't hear any of it—his selfishness utterly overruled his good judgment. Later on, of course, he could see that; at the time, he was completely blind to what his own greed and envy almost led him to do.

When the voice of selfishness pervades your inner critic, it can start talking you into justifications and rationalizations to do whatever you want, no matter who it hurts. When you're always lusting after more, you'll never be happy or at peace. That's because, in actuality, selfishness is the opposite of contentment. Some people will never be content with what they have. They will borrow, steal, or even kill to fulfill their desires.

To be content, on the other hand, is to inherently want more— it's human nature to want more—yet still be satisfied with what you have and who you are at present. Think of the Chinese principle of yin and yang. Elements must remain in balance to offset each other, to complement each other, to keep each other in check. It is when self-contempt, in turn, causes you to dislike and disdain everything around you. You can't enjoy your life at all when you spend it lusting after someone else's. That's no way to live—you don't want that voice perpetually in your head, egging you on to serve you and only you.

In the extreme, selfishness can give rise to narcissistic behaviors. Again, a certain amount of self-centeredness is understandable—it comes from our evolutionary past in which we had to take by any means necessary for our own survival. But we're not cave dwellers anymore who can allow all our thoughts and beliefs to be dictated by what we think we need for our own comfort. Take the idea of road rage. It astounds and fascinates me that some people believe they have been so violated by a fellow driver that it's perfectly justifiable to get caught up in a whirlwind of anger that can and has caused harm to self and others. That's the line of danger we shouldn't cross: when our self-focused, self-centered, self-entitled impulses and actions lead to hurting someone else. If you allow selfishness to overtake your conscience, you'll go after what you want without any thought or feeling for the people who will bear the brunt of your desires.

So what's the antidote to selfishness? What will tame the selfish voice that can easily get out of hand? Empathy, understanding and compassion. They make us humane, not merely human. We don't have to think less of ourselves to think more of others, to retrain the inner voice to focus more on considering what and who really matter to us in life instead of our own fleeting whims. I'll give the final word on this topic to author and biologist Richard Dawkins, because it's so fitting here: "Let us try to teach generosity and altruism, because we are born selfish. Let us understand what our own selfish genes are up to, because we might then at least have the chance to upset their designs, something that no other species has ever aspired to do."

The Voice of Objectivity

There's a natural order to the world out there. We might not see it as clearly when it comes to people in society, but we can easily see it when it comes to animals in the wild.

The wild that surrounds the veneer of civility humans inhabit can seem cruel to some, vital to others; structured or random; majestic or mundane. But it's a symphony that Mother Nature has been orchestrating over the course of time, and it's the same instruments that cause tsunamis to tower, volcanoes to blow, earthquakes to shake, floods to deluge, and droughts to devastate. But just as naturally and organically, rain can drench the savanna, rivers can be replenished, wildfires can be extinguished, skies can clear, and a safe haven can be found. A calm breeze in one part of the world can turn into a tornado elsewhere, but so too can the most threatening of hurricanes lose its power and dwindle above the ocean waters.

These are the laws of nature. The laws of nature are neither good nor bad. They just *are*. That's what the inner critic's voice of objectivity is like. It's neither good (like the voice of positivity) nor bad (like the voice of negativity), it just *is*. It lies between "right" and "wrong" in a territory of neutrality. It turns judgments into just statements, criticisms into observations. It replaces bias with balance, and both mud-washed and rose-colored glasses are wiped clean to allow for a clear vision of your path.

Laws in the wild are based on life-and-death instincts, senses, perceptions, survival mechanisms. So too are the laws that govern the voice of objectivity. It's a voiced that can be traced back to our ancestral roots as much as it can be traced back to last Tuesday. Instead of the parts of your inner critic that are buried in pains of the past or the parts that are prompted by your dreams for the future, the inner critic's objective voice speaks to you in and of the present—it assesses what's right in front of you, at this moment in your life, and creates a viewpoint that is neither in your rearview mirror nor off beyond the windshield. It has been schooled by your past and it thoughtfully considers how your present will affect your future, yes, but it is planted in the *here and now*, to help you make decisions *today*, as the person you are in this moment.

The voice of objectivity is the one you want to listen to when making choices about the direction of your life, about dilemmas you're currently facing. It helps you to decide if you want to move on or stay put, turn right or turn left, evolve or stay exactly as you are for the time being, because it's working for you. When you come to a challenging crossroads—a new job offer, whether to leave a relationship, to rent or buy, how to confront a friend who has disappointed you—your inner voice of objectivity is your mental partner in weighing the options and balancing the consequences so you can walk the best path for you at any given time.

It is your birthright to pursue your purpose, your calling, your dreams or vision for yourself. As you mature, you realize that procrastination doesn't serve you well, and neither does looking at all of life's options in a lackadaisical fashion. What is yours is waiting for you—and as often as not, it's not "out there," it's inside you. If you give power to the voice of objectivity inside you, it will be fed more and more by the positive aspect of your inner critic and less and less by the negative aspect. You will feel empowered to hurdle the obstacles that have been tripping you up and compelled to proudly claim what belongs to you, because the voice of objectivity can see the clear path forward to that place and time, to that healthy, thriving, balanced, and peaceful space inside you that can transform your whole life.

No matter what you're dealing with, you are greater than that current situation. You are. Whether you are battling depression, self-doubt, anxiety, or substance abuse, whether you're being held captive by the regrets of the past or paralyzed by fears for the future, you can break free, rise above, find new solid ground to stand on. There, the voice of objectivity will help you move forward, because it sees things for how they really are—it sees what is, not what you've subjectively interpreted it to be—and it can propose solutions as to what you can realistically do about it. It is up to you, not your spouse, not your parents, not your therapist, to make effective changes in your life by actively reframing your thoughts and behaviors.

Let's take a look at how to reframe your thoughts in an objective manner. Instead of applying the word "problem" to something you're currently going through, you can use the word "challenge." Reframing your language does a few things for you cognitively. The brain processes the information along different neuropathways. When you use the word "problem," you immediately have a physical reaction to the word. You might experience a stress response when you think about the problem: sweating, racing heartbeat, nervousness, jitters, dry mouth, or other physiological stress responses. Research has shown that more people die of heart attacks on Mondays. Why? Presumably because people are thinking about going back to stressful jobs they don't like or don't feel appreciated in.

The word "problem" makes it sound like it's something inside of you or that constitutes you, like you do not have control over the situation. *Boy, do I have a problem.* It just keeps coming up and knocking me down! When you accept that belief, you are limiting your options. But a "challenge" is something you encounter so you can learn from it, grow from it, conquer it, and thus gain strength over it. It is outside of you. It's an opportunity, not just a pitfall. *I've been presented with a challenge to resolve.* It is time to gain ground on meeting your potential in life by applying all your hard-earned experience and life lessons to inevitable challenges we'll all face.

Sure, you've made some significant mistakes and have probably burned a few bridges along the way, and although you can't go backward in time to undo them, you can move forward by putting positive energy back into the world and repairing whatever damage you can through forgiveness, honesty, truth, and love. Some people might not accept your apology, your explanation, whatever you offer them. You can come to the understanding that that is *their* choice— you've done what you can to make reparations. You don't have time or energy to spare to wait around for them to accept you or to show them over and over again how sorry you are by constantly trying to prove yourself to them. After the voice of objectivity has instilled in you what to do and say to make things right to the best of your ability in the present moment, you just have to accept that you've done your best and forgive yourself without hanging on to guilt and regret. The inner critic's negative voice would have you wandering in the desert of despair for years. But the objective voice will comfort and console you, telling you it's time to move on.

Black + White = Gray

Life isn't necessarily black and white. Things aren't 100 percent good or 100 percent bad. Very rarely is something all dark or all light. All right or all wrong. You'll never meet a person who is always an angel or always a devil. There's a vast area in between—the gray area that black and white form when considered in unison. Now, this area isn't necessarily the best in which to explore certain topics, like ethics. For example, if you start pondering stealing or cheating as a "gray area," you can very quickly descend into murky waters where you can either talk yourself into why you have a right to do something that you know is immoral or unfairly and subjectively judge someone else based on your own moral framework. But when we're talking about how to live life well and meaningfully, the gray area provides a lot of room for flexibility and space for consideration.

Say you have a choice to make—should you relocate your family for a promotion 1,800 miles away? If you make your choice based on one of two extremes—with only your own interests in mind or with only your children's interests in mind—there's a high likelihood that someone's going to suffer unwanted consequences of that choice. Questions like should you really move your family away from a happy existence when there might be a chance to find a better-paying or more fulfilling job right where you are? The gray area provides a place to negotiate, reach compromises, find solutions to issues that have direct and indirect consequences for both you and the people with whom you have relationships.

Similarly, you are not responsible for just yourself, and you are not the product of just other people's influences on you. There's a sliding scale in life in terms of accountability and influence. Parents are a good example of a varying amount of influence in our lives. If you didn't get the affection you craved from your parents, if your father didn't attend your practices or your mother was emotionally detached, you can choose to blame them entirely for anything and everything you're not happy with now. Or you can choose to deny that they have any power or sway over you now—now that you're an adult, out of their home, out of their grip.

The truth lies somewhere in between. You cannot escape the effects your early experiences had on you *and* you have the ability to live your adult life without letting those effects derail you from your chosen path. Each end point of the spectrum is valid, but you actually live real life along the continuum between those two extremes. Between these margins is where you find important insights that allow a deeper understanding of your relationships with others and yourself. It's where you discover what you're willing to tolerate and where you're willing to negotiate. You can better understand why teens make certain choices or adolescents give in to peer pressure because you yourself have lived through experiences that aren't just all this or all that, black or white. Your vault of experience on the sliding scale continuum of life will make you a better parent, partner, colleague, and friend. There are times when you will make choices for the greater good; there are times when you will prioritize the expression of your individuality.

The voice of objectivity lives in this gray area we've been talking about. As we go through life learning and evolving, you could even call this the voice of experience. It's particularly noticeable (and beneficial) in our professional and business lives, perhaps because these spheres aren't as emotionally charged as our romantic relationships and our family dynamics. We're able to be more objective at work because we've been hired to do a clear job there, and we're either good at it or we're not. If we perform poorly, we'll probably move on to something else that better suits us. But if we do well, if we stick with at least the same general career path for an extended period of time, we're exposed to situations and circumstances that we effectively and successfully manage, and the voice of objectivity stores that knowledge in our conscious mind and draws from when it's time to make the next decision.

An HR rep doesn't pick a résumé out of a hat and hire someone who used a nice typeface. His sense of objectivity will have informed him what to look for in a prospective employee, what traits that person's possible new boss values. A seasoned attorney will decide to take on a complex case based on what she's learned of such cases before: what moral dilemmas she may run into, what her fee structure should be, what the likelihood is that she will be able to deliver the outcome her client is seeking. An obstetrician isn't going to just stop in the middle of a difficult delivery and opt to do a C-section without having made that decision before and having gained a fuller understanding of the consequences and possible outcomes. Football players don't just run on the field and try to make touchdowns. They practice, they are coached, they study playbooks, they watch tape after tape to see what they'll be up against in the championship game, to see how they'll need to adapt styles and approaches in a particular circumstance.

It's the same in any area of life. This same process of impartial, informed assessment can and should apply equally to our personal lives—to all the choices we make every single day about how to plan, react, cope, behave, and think in relation to the world we live in and the people who live there with us. The voice of objectivity majorly draws from our experiences and acquired knowledge. To fortify that voice, we need to work hard and passionately to break out of a comfort zone that tells you you are right, the other person is wrong, this is the way something should be or should not be. Black and white thinking patterns might make it "easier" to decide something one way or the other, but they don't take into account the nuanced repercussions that can come from gut-reaction, inflexible decisions, dilemmas that are not as straight forward.

To live is easy. To live better requires effort. We need to study, practice, fine-tune, and then tune again our crafts, our interpersonal skills, and our roles in others' lives. People usually don't make business decisions based on subjective emotions—when to buy or sell stocks, when to invest in a company, what to charge or pay for a particular service. And so those decisions get more and more effective over time because we learn what normally works to our benefit and what normally doesn't. So why wouldn't we make other life decisions the same way—with the voice of reason and impartiality and fair assessment guiding our thoughts and actions? If the voice of objectivity works for you in your career, shouldn't it work for you elsewhere? How many times are you going to have the same argument with your spouse or partner? The voice of objectivity will help you to accurately apply wisdom and knowledge in these difficult, frustrating and complex relationship issues. If you replace a negatively charged voice of criticism and self-righteousness with one of equitable and even-handed neutrality aimed at problem-solving, you'll experience firsthand the inordinate power of the voice of objectivity.

One, Two, Three

The positive voice, the negative voice, and the voice of objectivity all try to influence our decisions—all our decisions, actually, the little ones as well as the big ones. The voices are always with us, so they are always filling our heads with sometimes conflicting thoughts, sometimes at the same time.

Take the simple example of dressing for work in the morning. As usual, you're in a hurry to get out the door, to beat the traffic and the line at Starbucks, but you have an important meeting today and so you want to look the part. You'd laid out your red tie last night, but now you're having doubts. It could be too bold—it could somehow send a message to Stephen that would scare him off the insurance plan you're selling him. Maybe you should switch to the blue tie—your wife says it brings out your eyes and you think it makes you seem more sedate and trustworthy. Then you wonder if you should stay away from red and blue altogether, given their political symbolism. Now, this isn't an ethical choice, it's not an important matter you're weighing. But your voices are at work all the same: Your worry that the red tie is an actual representation of yourself—that's the negative voice talking. This fuels anxiety provoking downward spiral thinking. Your confidence that you can earn your client's business by displaying your calmness and trustworthiness—that's your positive voice. In the end, you can't waste any more time on this little decision: It doesn't matter what you wear, all that matters is your performance at the meeting, so you just trust your original plan and head out the door in the red tie so you won't be late—that's the voice of objectivity.

Journal Time

We've covered a lot of ground in this chapter—not just the inner voice that speaks to you, but its three primary personas. I use real-life examples a lot to illustrate how psychological concepts play out in the real world, like the stories I relayed of Malcolm X or Ben Carson. Now it's time to turn to your real life and how these psychological concepts manifest for you in your daily life. So pull out your journal and spend some time answering these questions. The deeper you go, the more you'll learn about the nature and content of your own inner critic.

- Name at least three mental messages that you repeatedly hear that you know come from your voice of negativity. Next to each, write down where you think it originated.
- Name a regular thought you have that stems from self-doubt.
- Name a regular thought you have that stems from fear.
- Name a regular thought you have that stems from unappreciation of self.

- Name a regular thought you have that stems from selfishness.
- Name at least three mental messages that you repeatedly hear that you know come from your voice of positivity.
- Where you do think each of those messages originated?
- What's something positive you believe about yourself or the world based on actual experience?
- What's something positive you believe about yourself or the world based on just an inner knowing or faith in the idea?
- Now list a counterthought for each. (For example: *It doesn't matter what I say to Trina—she's mad at me and she's going to stay that way for a long time, like she usually does.* Counterthought: *I'm going to honestly tell her how I feel, take accountability for my part of the argument and explain how I felt about her part; regardless of how she responds, I'll feel better once I model healthy behavior and take a proactive step to heal our rift.*) Note: This is a good opportunity to implement *"I feel because statements"* that you learned in Chapter 3 under *language shifting* with the Derek and Lorinda example.
- Name at least three mental messages that you repeatedly hear that you know come from your voice of objectivity (*the voice of wisdom and knowledge*).
- Looking at those cognitions, is there an area of life in which you seem to use your objective voice most—at work, in parenting, with friends, when it comes to your physical fitness or finances?
- If so, how can you bring more of that type of thinking into other areas of your life? Be specific here—if you know the voice of objectivity governs you at work but not at home with your rebellious teenager, what particular techniques or strategies you use at work can you apply to improve your outcomes with your teen?
- Name an issue you're currently grappling with now. What is the negative voice telling you about it? What is the positive voice saying? What does the objective voice advise? Which

voice are you listening to the most? Which do you think you should listen to the most to best resolve the issue?

- Finally, where do you feel like God, the universe, or your higher power is leading you in terms of listening to the voice of positivity and the voice of objectivity? How do you feel like this will make you a better person, partner, husband, wife, father mother etc.?

CHAPTER 5

The Relationship Among the Three Voices

Growth occurs when individuals confront problems, struggle to master them, and through that struggle develop new aspects of their skills, capacities, views about life.

—Carl Rogers

The mind is a beautiful place where thoughts are formed through our own personal experiences. As I said earlier, some would equate the positive and negative voices of the inner critic to the good and bad, the angel and the devil, sitting on each of our shoulders. If so, the voice of objectivity can be likened to a passive observer listening to both sides of the conversation and weighing the potential outcomes of our choices. This sense of reasoning helps us successfully navigate through the world in which we live. We would not have survived as a species if we heeded *only* our negative critic or *only* our positive one—we require the ability of dispassionate thought to rationally judge the possible results of our own actions and the actions of others.

Ponder for a moment the last time you made a major life decision. What was that like for you? Was your inner voice telling you it was time to make a significant change in your life? Did you experience any type of anxiety—appetite changes, butterflies in your stomach, sleepless nights? Did you daydream? Before you made that decision, what was your mental voice telling you? Was it the voice of doubt? Of fear? Of logic?

Whether your thoughts were positive, negative, or reasoned in nature, the beauty of any decision-making experience is that it ultimately lies to you—the decision is ultimately yours to make. Coming to an understanding of the process of choice allows us a much greater sense of control over our lives. When we don't have this sense of control, we feel trapped. We get in situations that we do not enjoy. We often don't feel comfortable or safe. We feel as if the power of choice has been taken away from us.

This is no small matter. Wars have been fought over choice, over the compelling need for freedom. When we surrender this basic human need to an oppressor, we feel like we've been forced to go against our culture, standards, morals, or values—ultimately, we're devoid of a sense of oneness with ourselves. From the perspective of history, this has manifested as resistance, protest, civil wars, revolutions. This very country was founded on an unstoppable drive to free ourselves as a people from the perceived tyranny of a ruling authority overseas from whom we wanted our independence to live as we pleased, act as we pleased, govern ourselves as we pleased. From the perspective of your everyday life, when your sense of selfhood and your own moral codes are compromised, it can lead to unwanted stress or depression. When we don't live by our own choices, anxiety goes up at the very thought of what we have to face today, tomorrow, or in the near future.

Fear and stress go hand in hand, affecting our overall health. Recall that most heart attacks occur on Monday mornings between the hours of six a.m. and noon. Many people wake up to a stressful situation they neither want nor like: a demanding boss, passive-aggressive coworkers, a workload that's too intense or unreasonable. I have counseled numerous people who feel no break from their stress because they're going to bed with it on their minds and they're waking to it—to the reality that their problem has not gone anywhere. It is a ghost that refuses to leave, haunting every aspect of their life and therefore causing them to live in perpetual fear. Throughout the day, they cannot enjoy their activities, the weather, the small blessings, their families. Their families might even be the source of the stress. So where do they find a break? Some people just go psychologically numb. They go through the motions of daily living, but they are checked out. This is the mind's way of dealing with an overwhelming situation that seems to be out of one's control.

A large part of the population is dependent on medication and frequent doctor visits to treat depression and anxiety. Not to say that there is no need for psychiatric drugs. This doesn't have to be the case where you are solely dependent on them for a complete answer to your problems—you are greater than this! You don't have to die an early death (literally or figuratively) or to live a life that is less than what you want for yourself. If you want to decrease your stress, anxiety, or depression, it's time to make some significant changes in your life. *You* have to make that choice to change things; no one else can make that decision for you, and my goal here is to get you to see that the choice always has been yours. Yes, you need to come to an accurate understanding of whatever challenge you're facing before you can be guided toward resolving it—with the help of a therapist like me, if you wish—but you *can* find resolution. If your current state isn't working for you, it's time to address some difficult choices and make some hard decisions. A combination of your negative voice, positive voice, and objective voice can help you do that.

The Job of the Positive Critic

The paramount mission of the positive critic is to turn bad or unfortunate experiences into good ones—it has the will to do that. Although it can't erase or undo abuses or horrible events in your life, it can transform even the most harrowing of experiences into learning opportunities, into life lessons that will ultimately enrich your life and enlighten your soul. In any decision-making process, the positive critic is always available to guide you; so it's imperative to give it the power, space, opportunity, and wherewithal to speak to you. Try as you might, you will not be able to completely silence the negative or critical voice through substances—you can contaminate the mind with drugs and alcohol to suppress inner pain, to temporarily fog and blur uncomfortable thoughts, but you cannot eliminate this negative inner voice. So, the best approach, the healthiest approach, is to lasso your potential and learn to use your past experiences in your favor.

How? How do we increase the volume of the positive voice, decrease the volume of the negative voice, and give the balancing voice in between more room to roam and explore. This is an age-old question that philosophy and the arts have been analyzing for centuries, though they might use different language than how we're discussing these issues now.

In the Bible, the Apostle Paul talked about the inner war raging inside him between good and evil. It was a constant struggle within him. On a day-to-day basis, he felt like he was being torn one way or the other. He went so far as to refer to the experience as a kind of "death." It's an interesting dichotomy—the internal battle between doing what is good for us and giving ourselves over to our negative energies or baser instincts. Some would argue that there is no true evil—just choice and existence. I don't necessarily believe this. To me, good and evil are evident just by taking a look at the world around us. Whether or not good and evil truly exist and whether we actually have a choice in the matter would make for a good debate, but that's not the point here!

The point is that Paul's internal war is something we can all relate to. Have you ever found yourself in a predicament where you were struggling between two moral absolutes? We often feel trapped within the decision-making process when the choices we have to make are difficult. Choosing between two equally attractive apartments isn't all that difficult; choosing between two equally attractive, but different, potential mates is much more complicated. The dilemma lies in the fact that there is no one perfect choice. No clear-cut, ideal answer that will hold true under all conditions. If you give up Layla to pursue a relationship with Regina, you have to give up Layla's offbeat sense of humor, her steady career, her sexy legs, her talent on the piano; but if you give up Regina to pursue a relationship with Layla, you have to give up Regina's intelligence, her way with people, her brilliant smile, her financial savvy.

So we circle back here to the idea of the gray world in between the black and white. We're conflicted when we feel pressured to go one way and only one way. Your negative critic will keep reminding of you what you've got to lose, that things will turn sour if you make the wrong decision, of the regret and remorse that lie ahead. *I want them both! I don't want to lose either Layla or Regina! God, why can't I ever figure things out? What's wrong with me? No matter what I choose, I lose.* (Translation: fear, doubt, selfishness, unappreciation of self.) Your voice of objectivity, in contrast, will advise you to realistically assess the pros and cons of each relationship, to not be led solely by your emotions because they can change but to identify solid, rational, pragmatic reasons to be with one or the other: *Which temperament is better suited to mine? Who do I have more in common with? Who wants to live in the same place I do and aspire to similar goals? What are her dreams? What are her passions? Are we on the same wave length? Do I enjoy her presence? Does she compliment me? Is it easy to date her and be with her? How many kids does this one want? How many bad habits does that one have? Does she make me a better person?* If one of these relationships does not work out the voice of positivity can be your best friend in such instances. It can also comfort you with the knowledge that you can be happy with either decision, that a win-win is possible; by assuring you that you're going to be okay either way and that you made the best choice you could at the time with the information you had available.

The end goal is to make healthy, forward-looking decisions that are mutually beneficial for all involved parties, giving due consideration to the legitimate concerns of all parts of the inner critic. But it's not easy to make the healthiest choices in the presence of clashing yearnings, is it?

So we need to reconcile the struggles existing within us. There are multiple options to do so. Some find resolution and peace in religion—in their religious beliefs, they find the guidance they need to move forward with confidence and fortitude. Some find it in spirituality—through deep inner work and a continuous striving toward something beyond the corporal and the mundane, they discover the means to hold on to their balance and perspective when the world rattles them. Some teach themselves to reconcile their struggles through self-help exercises, through education, through therapy, or through support networks of friends and fellows. And some learn to tame their inner demons and let their higher selves prevail in acts of service—as they help others in need, they discover how best to help themselves. All of these options, and more, are available to you.

We are all seeking purpose and meaning. This inherent tendency, I believe, leads us to do good and be good even when we didn't think we knew what was good for us. Think of all the acts of heroism and altruism that sprout up in glorious numbers when we're faced with crisis and tragedy. The selfless acts of men and women on 9/11. The relief teams that rally in the wake of natural disasters. Volunteer search parties. People who take in stray pets; people who house foreign exchange students. The police officers, firefighters, first responders, and various other civil servants who regularly risk their lives to save others. Ladies auxiliaries and elks lodges that host fundraisers for community families. Everyone in the medical field; all the helping professions. The act of paying it forward. Paying for the car behind you. Lending a hand to someone who's struggling in a store or out in public. Goodness and positivity are all around us all the time. It doesn't appear out of thin air—people create it by choosing to act honorably and charitably.

Yes, the fear and doubts that comprise the negative voice mutter in our ear to save ourselves, to run for shelter, to look away ... each man for himself, dog eat dog. Life is hard enough—do we really need to fight even more and work even harder toward personal growth? Can't we just give ourselves a break and take the easy way out? Well, you can, I suppose, but then you'd be surrendering to the negative thought processes in your head, and, ironically, that makes life even harder. When we observe the world through the lens of the negative critic, it is harder to see our own capabilities and talents, harder to accept things as they are, harder to live in an unavoidably imperfect world. Everything and everyone is flawed in some way. We all have shortcomings and things that frustrate us. The negative critic focuses on these deficits; it stays mired in the problems instead of swimming toward solutions. But the beauty of humanity stems from imperfections, from our constant striving toward something more— the beauty is intertwined with our hurt, pain, shame, and insecurity. We all feel these things, though some to greater degrees.

Maybe you've been ridiculed for being socially awkward, weird, strange, or different. Maybe you were bullied to the point of being brought to tears. Maybe you were criticized by your parents so much that you had to or still need to wholly redefine your self-concept, self-esteem, and self-confidence. Whatever road you've traveled thus far—however bumpy it's been or how much smoother it is now that you've been able to overcome some early harshness—we all come to a turning point where we have to decide to proactively plow ahead or stand still, remain stuck. So many people are stuck.

But you know what? I believe every one of us has good in us—knows what it means and what it feels like to be good and do good. And that means we all have the potential to make positive choices for ourselves and for others. It's the voice of the positive inner critic that compels us to do that—to make better choices for ourselves as we journey along and to cultivate altruism toward others as we do so. It is up to us to tune in to this voice. It's often stifled by our own personal biases and prejudices that drown out our moral code and our inclination to act for the greater good. But if we listen more closely and more often to it, the positive critic is trying to persuade us to follow its advice and take action. Life has meaning, purpose. The positive critic desires to lead you in the direction of your own meaningfulness and purposefulness. Each time you heed its call, it's your negative inner critic that gets drowned out instead and you're one step closer to a fruitful life filled with passion and abundance.

Rehabbing the Mind by Restructuring Inner Thoughts

The way out of "stuckness" begins with understanding how the mind functions. Humans are unique among all other species on the globe. We are conscious of our place in the world and we have the ability to look within. This singular quality has its perks and its setbacks. Looking into ourselves gives us the opportunity to develop a way of thinking that allows us to understand who we truly are as individuals. With this understanding, you can make the conscious choice to improve your inner self.

In the same manner, you have the choice to ignore or suppress deep-seated issues. In working with many clients over the years, I've seen this phenomenon cause numerous difficulties within the relationships people long for and seek. You can only suppress inner issues for so long before they begin to ooze into your work, your style of communication, how you treat your partner, how you raise your children, and how you treat yourself.

As we venture along the rabbit trail and eventually down the rabbit hole, we find that there are several layers to the emotional self. Like Alice in Wonderland, when you venture down into your inner self, you will come across many characters who have defined and affected the way you think about yourself and how you behave toward others.

Do you remember the caterpillar that Alice comes across in Wonderland? He asks her a simple question that packs a profound punch. Taking a big puff from his "cigarette holder," he asks, "Who are you?" The caterpillar is not asking her her name. He's not asking her about her age or where she lives or what her hobbies are. He's provoking her to contemplate her inner self. Our beliefs about who we are and how we choose to act on those beliefs are in many ways shaped by the interactions that have affected us emotionally.

As conscious beings, we must all ask ourselves at some point, "Who am I?" Many people simply don't know or plod through life trying to find the answer. The inner search for meaning begins with that question. How you relate to other people, how you attach or detach with those you love, how you conceptualize success and happiness, how you come to terms with your emotional baggage, with codependency issues, how you work (or don't work) through your "unfinished business"—all of this is part of amassing a greater understand of the inner self.

Most emotional insecurity has been molded by our caregivers. In your experience with your parents or caregivers and how they chose to raise you, were your interactions with them mostly positive, mostly negative, or somewhere in between? As we've already learned, it is here in our earliest encounters that the voice of the inner critic originates. The sum of our interactions with our parents is then expanded by interactions with other influential people in our lives, up to the present moment. The inner critic continues to be fed by both the positive and negative messages you've heard, but it's also heavily influenced by the way you process these messages and internalize them. These messages later evolve into themes, which are a result of often-faulty beliefs that interfere with emotional progress. For example, the inner dialogue of a theme might be saying, *I am not good enough, I am not strong enough,* or *I am not smart enough.* When you believe this faulty inner theme, when you act on it, it can give rise to "stuckness," loneliness, isolation, insecurity, social awkwardness, and emotional stagnation.

It is incredibly difficult to rescript the story of our lives when we were raised in an environment not conducive to positive growth. It's also difficult to rescript the story of our lives when we're currently, as adults, living in an environment not conducive to positive growth.

Still, if you have the courage to travel farther down Alice's rabbit hole, you will find that you have the choice to believe the negative or positive messages you've internalized to be true, false, or somewhere in between; you have the choice to accept or reject the themes that have emerged from the messages.

If you were told as a child or if you are still being told as an adult that you are nothing and will not amount to anything, you can choose to believe this and behave in ways that reinforce this, or you can challenge yourself to prove the message false. When we're little, we don't have much agency in the matter, because we are emotionally, financially, and physically dependent on our caregivers for our very survival. Actually, we're emotionally dependent on them for the foundation of our self-esteem and self-concept, too. But if you're old enough to have gotten your hands on this book because it's relevant to you and you're looking for answers, then you *do* have agency now—you *do* have power to work through negative inner messages about yourself that you either knowingly or unknowingly accepted and incorporated.

Remember what I told you at the start? You are the author of your own story—you *can* rewrite it. This doesn't change the events that transpired, but it does reframe them in such a way that your story becomes yours to steer and direct, something you are proud of, something from which you've learned and grown, something you can share with the world to make it a better place and to increase your own quality of life.

We can and we must redefine ourselves by discarding negative labels that have been placed on us by others or even ourselves—labels like FAILURE, WEAK, INADEQUATE, LOSER. Deep down, you *know* that's not true—you know the negative critic is just trying to intimidate and defeat the positive critic. You *know* you have a choice to believe one more than the other. Choose to believe in yourself! Accept that right this minute is the perfect time to start shifting your life in the direction you want to go. Stop living according to other people's conceptions of you and conceive a new you for yourself! Restructure the play of your life so that you become the hero, not the victim. Because that's what you are: You are your own hero, savior, advocate— you are your story's protagonist. And the protagonist is responsible for moving the story forward. Reframing your personal narrative might just be the most worthwhile endeavor you ever undertake.

Embracing Our Imperfections

Protagonists aren't perfect, of course. They act and they execute, they push and they pull, but they make mistakes along the way. But that lifelong companion of yours, that positive inner critic allows you to embrace your imperfections as gifts, because it's from them—from your missteps, not your victories—that you mature and evolve. Once we learn to work through and adapt to the challenges that come our way, we begin to see the results of putting our so-called imperfections to work for us. I believe that true ingenuity arises from one's failures. How many times did Nikola Tesla fail in his experiments before he bestowed on the world life-changing inventions and advancements born only of his own visions and dreams for himself and others?

You are the accumulation of your trials, errors, successes, and failures. They are all wrapped into a beautiful, one-of-a-kind human being. Don't let good opportunities pass you up by focusing on how imperfect you are or on what you don't have. The negative inner critic will have you believe that you messed up and that tomorrow won't be any better. The negative inner critic will have you wallowing in self-pity. Could you have made better choices? Absolutely. Could you have made choices that didn't burn bridges behind you? Yes. But ask yourself the important questions: What did these choices teach you? How will you avoid these pitfalls in the future? How have you built upon your past experience to offer the world a greater you?

It is of the utmost importance to have a victor mentality and not a victim mentality. When you see yourself as a victim, you're not only at a psychological disadvantage, you're the one who's put yourself there. When someone perpetrates harm on others, their world begins to close up—their choices become limited. When you see yourself as victorious, however, as someone who has forgiven yourself your faults and has the grace to forgive others, the world begins to open up to you. The voice of objectivity allows you to weigh your options. By looking at an argument from both positive and negative angles, the inner critic allows us to have a greater sense of autonomy and free will. The negative and the positive inner critic will never force you to make a choice. But based on what they're telling you, it is up to you to make that conscious choice.

You are the master of choice. It is what you do with this choice that determines the outcome of your life's journey. That's why it's very difficult for us to assess the success of others. Everybody is on their own path. Social media, television, YouTube—we use them as portals to look over the fence at someone else's life and imagine their garden is so much more plentiful than our own. Your garden might have twigs, branches, and weeds in it, it's true. But you can cultivate your own garden in your own time—it's up to you to do that. With the proper tools, time, effort, and tenacity, you can grow a garden that will produce a bountiful harvest.

It's easy to look with envious eyes at those with fame and fortune who take champagne baths and attend grand parties every weekend. In comparison, your life doesn't just seem imperfect, it seems downright disappointing. But you don't know what's under there if you scratched the surface and looked beneath: Rich, beautiful people have emptiness, hurt, pain, and unresolved issues too. Money and celebrity don't bring happiness—not true happiness, anyway. You want your life to be filled with truth, honesty, and genuineness. So go after what you want, even if it means digging in the dirt and biding your time for a while. The reward will be worth the sacrifice and effort. Usually, that's what it takes.

Dr. Carl Rogers once said, "The good life is a process, not a state of being. It is a direction, not a destination." Your process might take longer than someone else's. Your process might not be as pretty—it might be outright ugly at times!—but it's yours. You own it, you and you alone; you were meant to have it, it is both your birthright and your legacy. Your process will take blood, sweat, and tears, a lot of hard work, determination, and grit. You will face letdowns, prejudice, racism, sexism, ageism, judgment, and rejection. This is all part of the process, and so you've got to embrace it all. And when you come out of the refiner's furnace, you will come out as pure gold. The refiner's fire welds your will, brands your character, and ignites your talents.

CHAPTER 6

Actionable Steps to Confront and Defeat the Negative Inner Critic

My mother did not want me. So I focused within for my sense of security. Even in my darkest days, I realized that when I sincerely strove to help myself and kept a peaceful, hopeful outlook, magical things happened. Eventually, I was able to heal my heart and give myself the love I hadn't received when I was young. I like to say that I changed the poison into medicine and transformed the difficulties in my life to realize my dreams.

—Tina Turner

Alex Zanardi was born in Bologna, Italy. The son of Dino and Anna Zanardi began racing at thirteen. A creative kid, he built his first go-cart from the wheels of a dustbin and pipes from his father's workplace. He started his career in Formula 1 auto racing in 1991–1994, then added sports car racing to his repertoire. Paired with Alex Portman, he managed to finish fourth at a wet-weather race at Silverstone. He had his first CART win at Laguna Seca during the 1996 season, when he overtook the leader at the Corkscrew corner with a very risky and dangerous move called the "Pass," which was later banned.

Unfortunately, in 2001, Zanardi suffered a violent crash at the EuroSpeedway Lausitz, resulting in the loss of three-quarters of his blood volume and both of his legs (one at the knee and the other at the thigh). Although he survived the three-hour surgery immediately following his accident, his legs had to be further amputated during the procedure.

This was supposed to be the end of the road for Zanardi, but he was a notorious fighter. Outfitted with prosthetic limbs he designed himself, he fought through the pain of rehab and the trauma of losing his legs. By 2003, he was able to return to racing and went on the enjoy the sport he loved for years to come, also becoming a paracyclist along the way.

What would have become of Alex Zanardi if he'd just succumbed to the negative voice? To the voice that will chide us for our recklessness, caution us against taking risks, and just accept what others tell us to accept? When Zanardi's initial prostheses weren't working for him, he devised a custom solution that would allow him to still engage in his passion. What perseverance and tenacity that must have taken! Not all of us will face the level of hardship Zanardi did from his hospital bed, not all of us will be called on to display the amount of courage he needed to get back up. Over and over again. But we can all understand the depression, fear, self-doubt, and other forms of destructive energy that can take root in the mind when the negative critic is at its most powerful.

In this form, the negative critic goes all out to make us feel lesser than we are. It commences a war—the most pernicious kind of war there is: the one against the self, the one that holds us captive from the inside. If that war is lost ... well, we can't lose that war. Each individual must fight tooth and nail to defeat the internal critic's onslaught of self-doubts and barrage of self-sabotaging and self-destructive tendencies when they emerge at the lowest points in our lives. We must battle relentlessly against any entity, force, or vessel that tries to infuse counterproductive energy into our souls. If Zanardi can do it without legs, you can do it with two. The fifteen actionable steps mapped out in this chapter will help you tame the destructive voice of negativity in your mind so that it's just a pesky nuisance the opposing positive voice learns to swat down and shut up.

Rooting Out Your Own Negative Critic

Before we dive into the actions you can take to conquer your negative critic, it's important that you are very clear on the nature and characteristics of your own, because the first step in beating any problem is to identify the problem. The people who feel like prisoners in a world of negativity are usually the people who haven't yet pinpointed why and how they got there.

The negative critic is indeed a problem, but its source is a bigger problem—even if you take away the voice, you'll still be left with the root, and the root grows into new offshoots over time. We've already talked a good deal about where the negative inner voice comes from, so let's take a look now into its levels, of which there are two: (1) the negative voice from the superficial and (2) the negative voice from the deep.

The superficial negative voice is easy to identify and easy to defeat. That's because it's very close to the surface, easily accessible to you and easy to relate to. For example, a woman with a poor body image knows exactly why she's low in confidence in this area: She doesn't like the freckles on her face and her weirdly long legs. She can easily identify the negative voice's root here—the thought that she is ugly—her surface root would bring up thoughts and feelings associated with the deeper root such as anxiety, irritability, anger, frustration, envy, worry, and jealousy. Her deeper root or "core beliefs" would be linked to assumptions like she is not good enough, or worthlessness, uncertainty insignificance, inadequacy, and insecurity. Once the deeper root is addressed and cut off, she can begin to find ways to feel more attractive and hold herself in higher regard. Another example: A man feels sad and envious looking out the window at his neighbor's new boat. His mind tells him he's an underachiever, a low performer, that he'll never catch up to where other people are. His core beliefs about himself are indeed negative and are further triggered by his neighbor's new purchase—the surface root here would be envy, jealousy, anger, depression, feeling irritable, frustrated, confused and disappointed. His deeper roots would be feelings of regret, resentment, fear, and emptiness.

The negative voice from the deep is more dangerous. The danger lies in the fact that its victims might not realize that they are suffering from the consequences of a deeper issue. Some people are unhappy, but they might not know it or have any idea why. Others are inherently angry, yet they will deny the temper so obvious to the outside world. Others have low self-esteem that keeps them from living their fullest lives, but they're not even aware that that's their stumbling block.

Take another woman who regards herself in a poor light and doesn't even know she's a victim of some sort of injustice. This woman never feels comfortable taking a leading role or expressing herself in predominantly male gatherings. She cares too much about what other people think, and although she loves engineering, she's never taken upper-level classes because she feels incapable of learning anything. She is never adventurous—her inner cheerleader, if she even has one, never encourages her to take a chance. She is bound by her limiting thoughts that are governed by her core beliefs.

Now, there are many possible reasons why this woman has such low self-esteem, many possible roots: She may have been raised in a society that thinks less of women; if so, that's her culture and that's what she knows. She may have been dominated by a domineering father or married a man who projected his inner demons onto her thus *silencing* her voice. This form of psychological abuse would lead her to believe that his demons were her own or that they were her fault. She may not have been nurtured and supported by her caregivers, so she doesn't feel worthy of that. She may have lost a sibling at a young age, which would make the world a very unsafe place for her, or been sexually assaulted by someone. She is then be chained by fear, doubt and uncertainty. Or maybe the assault happened to someone else, like her mother, who never fought back and thus never modeled self-respect self-confidence, self-respect and self-defense to her daughter. Whatever the cause, at forty-five years of age, this woman is not anything more than witnessed, experienced or what she was told she could be. Without intervention, this woman might live in mental bondage for the rest of her life without even realizing it.

As we've discussed, it's essential to objectively assess our lives every now and then so that we *do* realize, we *are* aware, we know what to confront. This may require you to root out a few repressed memories, feelings, or experiences. You can have a professional help you, someone who can perhaps see some things you can't see about your life patterns, your identity, your negative-thought-provoked behaviors and actions. The right questions must be asked, questions like:

- Do I really believe I'm ugly? If I do is it because of societies standards of beauty? Social media? What others have said to me?
- Do I believe I deserve the good things of life? If I don't then why?
- Do I feel like success is beyond my reach? Why?
- Do I yearn for a fuller, richer life?
- Am I just accepting the mediocre life I lead?

Journal in hand, exploring these questions might begin to evoke some repressed or forgotten memories so that you can begin to understand *why* you've answered the way you have. You might begin to understand why you remain in an abusive relationship or why you yourself physically or mentally abuse the people around you. Some of the negativities in your life will be traced to your childhood, some to faulty societal values, or church or school or relationships, among other experiences. The important thing is to keep tracing back, all the way to the root, so you can eventually pluck the weeds and allow your blossoms to flourish.

Step #1: Tell Yourself the Exact Opposite of What the Negative Critic Tells You

The mind's constant thought cycle operates on both positive and negative levels. When a negative occurrence (relationship, communication, or experience) happens, it can be turned into a negative thought pattern that in turn gives rise to a new negative message uttered by the negative critic. The negative critic can then incite someone to act out in negativity. The negative action will produce another negative experience that will produce another negative thought pattern.

Real-life example: A man was repeatedly told by his father that he would never amount to anything. This formed a core belief and a negative thought pattern in his mind. His core belief was he was didn't have any value, he was unworthy, and incapable. His inner voice told him he wouldn't succeed at college anyway, so he dropped out. Dropping out of college led to an unfulfilling job he didn't like, and this experience echoed in his mind as: *I'm stuck in a loop I can't get out of—I'm not going to be able to advance in life.* So he stays in the same dead-end job for ten years just to keep a roof over his head, lacking the positive outlook to branch out and pursue more for himself. All the while, he has supported his father's assertions, proving them true.

Negativity is a seed planted in the fertile ground of the mind. That one seed grows into a tree that bears fruits, which themselves bear more seeds, which grow into trees. The seed of one negative thought has the capacity to bear *hundreds* of other negative thoughts. It's an exponential formula.

Combating the process entails persistent resistance to that harmful mental chatter—constant assertions of the exact opposite of what the negative thought is expressing in your head. If the negative thought is *I'm a failure,* then the constant counterassertion must be words of victory: *I am not a failure. Yes, I've failed in some enterprises and I'm not where I want to be yet, but I'm not a failure. I've learned from these mistakes. They have made me the powerful person I am today! I can succeed on my own terms and I have plenty of time to succeed! I will be on top!*

Positive assertions and affirmations neutralize negative energy, disarm it. Starve the beast of negativity by refusing to heed its words. Feed the powerful lion of positivity by consistently asserting positive words to yourself.

Words are powerful enough to influence our decisions and beliefs. When words are constantly invoked in our mind's ear, we will act out those words. Every person has some negativity. Search for your negative energies and the negative words and experiences that feed these energies and then vehemently and constantly confront them with positive beliefs and actions. Let the power that is within you not be held back by limiting beliefs and thoughts. Speak your success and freedom into existence!

Step #2: Know Your Word

There are particular words for particular moments, particular situations. A thousand negativities can be deflected with just a single word, statement, or positive assertion that you devise for that purpose. A shipwreck survivor held on to a pole for three days at sea until the rescue team found her. When she was asked how she was able to survive such an impossible ordeal, she said she held on to the thought that her daughter was due to give birth in a month—she wasn't going to miss that moment for anything. The thought of seeing her grandchild was the "word" she spoke for every minute of the three days she stayed at sea without food or potable water.

When things go wrong, as they sometimes do—when you

are flooded with doubt and fear—you need a word or phrase of encouragement that will spark your will and ride you through the tide. This word can be sourced from the things that mean the most to us. A businessman in Los Angeles suffered great losses during the recession in 2008. His company hung on a thread, and at one point, he had to work for a rival company to make ends meet. Three years later, he had bounced back and expanded his company to four times its original value. When he was asked how he'd managed the crisis— and the accompanying embarrassment that came with it—he replied, "What I do isn't just for the money. Money is important and profit is good, but in the absence of profit, I still do what I have to do because I love doing it. I love this business. Take it all away, and I will remain here working on my job." That's what got him through—that mantra, that belief system: "Because I love what I do!" Songs of Solomon 8:7 in the Berean Study Bible says, "Many waters cannot quench love, nor can rivers drown it. If a man tried to buy love with all his wealth, his offer would be utterly scorned."

People have risen out of poverty and against great odds to pursue and achieve their life goals. A writer who is truly committed will not stop after a few rejected submissions or a low-selling first novel. She will keep writing and writing and writing—working, improving and knowing that her work *will* reach prominence someday. I remember hearing Denzel Washington praise a young producer's perseverance in one of his speeches. The young man self-produced more than fifteen short series before he was finally given the chance to work on a big project. His belief in himself and his passion would not allow him to give up. Likewise, an aspiring actor will audition and audition. He will hone his craft. He will sleep in the park if he has to. He knows that someday, far or near, he will get his big shot.

Self-doubt and fear can be combated with a word for the moment. Search your soul, find your jewels there, and you will find your word. I have found what I love to do, and in the presence of turmoil, doubt, and fear, I do what I have to do because I love what I do. No one is exempt from hardship; it is what we do with the hardship that makes all the difference. Falling in love and being passionate about an occupation or vocation makes the hard times easier because we are not compelled or forced to do work we do not like. What are you passionate about? What drives you? What is your motivating factor?

Find what you're cut out for. Not everyone is cut out to be a therapist—working with various forms of human behavior and mental processes can cause burnout on the first day. In my case, I discovered I wasn't cut out for the medical field when I had to get my blood drawn for my trip to Kenya. When the nurse called my name, I immediately felt the nervousness in my stomach and sweat broke out on my forehead. The nurse was very polite as she was preparing for the blood draw, but I could barely hear a word she was saying above my heartbeat inside my chest. When she asked me to raise my sleeve, I knew not to look down—all I had to do was not look down. So what did I do? I looked down. Then I felt lightheaded and saw the world closing around me. The last thing I remember was seeing a small light at the end of that tunnel and thinking, *This is it!*

When I woke up after the first time in my life I'd ever fainted, the nurse and a doctor were standing over me and trying to give me some air. To deal with the shame, I had to keep reminding myself that this was all for a noble cause: to meet my grandparents. I know now that I can't look at my own blood going into a tube just as surely as I know that I found the right profession.

Knowing our strengths and familiarizing ourselves with our capabilities will help us move toward the one thing that really lights our fire. And when times get tough, just keep telling yourself over and over why you're doing it.

Step #3: Venture into Unfamiliar Territory

When we grow in our personal and professional lives, we enter new territories. Growth requires facing bigger and more complicated challenges, trying new things, acquiring new skills. The way to conquer fears of the mind is to just start bulldozing through them, at whatever pace is comfortable to you, to get to the other side of them. Some people balk under the pressure and fail to overcome their fears, but we all have the ability to at least test them, if not prove them wrong, if we're willing to venture into unknown terrain.

Consider friends Aaron and Stuart. Aaron's a thirty-five-year-old entrepreneur who wanted to expand his business, but he was afraid of talking to investors. His business model was sound and he'd been turning a profit for two years, but the thought of presenting to investors just scared him off. He saw them as demigods almost, as more than mere mortals, and his doubting critic told him they'd never be interested in his plan.

Stuart told him something different, though. Stuart's dad had worked with investors for years and that industry didn't intimidate him in the least. If Aaron had to rely on investors for his business to grow, then he was resigned to just stick to how things were, but Stuart prodded him to not settle for that. Stuart was able to convince Aaron to move out of his comfort zone and arranged a first meeting for his friend with one of his father's contacts. When Aaron finally did face his fears, he realized they'd been out of proportion—pitching to investors wasn't much different than pitching to clients: Both were people who had money he wanted. Within six months, he pitched to three different groups of investors, becoming more and more confident each time.

Stuart didn't doubt himself in business—Stuart's weak area was romance. The first time he saw Andrea at the restaurant where she worked, he fell in love with her, but he was no ladies' man and had never so much as spoken to her. When he confided this to Aaron, Aaron decided to return Stuart's favor by helping him out with Andrea. The two of them went over scenarios for weeks—what Stuart could say to her to break the ice, how he could get a conversation going. They role-played multiple times and discussed possible outcomes. They agreed that the worst that could possibly happen was that she'd never speak to him again—and that seemed highly unlikely.

Stuart finally got the courage to ask Andrea out and she accepted. She seemed very pleased with the effort he'd put into the date—the restaurant he chose, the flowers he brought her, his gentlemanly manners—and admitted she'd noticed him too and had hoped he'd talk to her. They had a lovely date, and when he kissed her good night at her door, they made plans to see each other again.

The unknown sometimes seems mythical and mysterious, beyond our reach. And that can spark fears and doubts that speak to us in ways that limit us and stop us from pursuing our goals. If Aaron had let that negative self-talk inhibit his progress, he never would have gotten to the next level in his career. And if Stuart had continued to accept the inner belief that he had no game with women, he wouldn't be in a relationship with Andrea now.

Fear of failure is one of the major causes of accepting mediocrity, especially among students. I have worked with some students who were so afraid of failing that they were paralyzed by academic anxiety. They allowed the fear to override rational thought, and once it dominated their college experience, it permeated other aspects of their lives. Negative thought patterns in one area can easily migrate to other areas. And it hardly matters if the faulty belief isn't true, isn't based on any evidence. People can take purely hypothetical scenarios and convince themselves they're true—they write a script of failure before even trying to overcome what they fear will happen, and before you know it, they are actors in their own sad stories, with the negative inner critic as the director.

You don't have to let that happen. Instead, you can take one single step onto a stage that feels scary and unfamiliar ... and then just keep taking one small step at a time until the territory becomes more familiar and you eventually start commanding it.

Step #4: Debunk Faulty Beliefs

Your inner critic says inside, *You never win at anything.* So you say on the outside, "I can't beat him. He's six feet tall and the best wrestler here. I don't stand a chance."

Your inner critic says, *You're not smart enough.* So you go into class saying, "I can't pass this exam—it's too hard for me."

Your inner critic says, *You're not good-looking.* So you turn away from Michelle at the dance: "She's too pretty for me. I can't get someone at that level."

You hear such thoughts in your mind when you've already accepted their validity, when you've bought into a prewritten script laden with faulty beliefs about yourself. Each time you act on those beliefs, you're feeding the negative inner critic more energy, more power over the decisions you make. You might even think you're telling yourself the truth.

Granted, we do have limitations, there are some things we're not good at, and not everyone has movie-star good looks. But you can't decide what's true on the basis of how you feel emotionally because emotions change—they're highly influenced by subjectivity. And you don't want to just accept things as false—for example, it's false to believe that you're not smart because others told you so when you were held back in fourth grade—without enough actual lived experience and evidence to bear out their claims. It might be true that you're not a straight A student, but then most people aren't. Does that mean you're going to fail every test, turn in subpar papers semester after semester, have a totally unsatisfying academic career? No, of course not. But it does mean that you're probably going to have to work harder than some of the other students. That you might have to spend more hours studying in the library. That you should turn off the television, put down the phone, and do the work that needs to be done to get the results you want.

Most people in this world don't have it easy. Believing everyone else is just smoothly sailing along while we struggle is just another faulty belief that lets us feel sorry for ourselves instead of holding ourselves accountable to achieve more. Successful people are the ones who have worked hard, persevered, put in the extra time, sacrificed, gone through the pain of getting up after failing, learned from challenges, and used their time wisely. They didn't just snap their fingers and—*poof!*—the world was served to them on a silver platter.

Your job, if you want to defeat the negative critic that is holding you back from success, is to follow the lead of the people you admire and want to emulate, by learning the ropes of the ring you want to play in, just like they did. You start at the beginning, and then you train and you study and you learn and you apply yourself until you achieve what you want to achieve. Calculus starts with elementary mathematical computations; masterpieces are written on a foundation of the ABCs; quantum physics cannot be grasped without a basic understanding of biology and chemistry. To think you're not capable of something because you can't master it out of the gate is as misguided as thinking someone can be a brain surgeon without going to med school. All of us must slowly and steadily acclimate to unfamiliar surroundings before tackling more complicated matters.

Don't be misled or disillusioned by what you see on Facebook, Instagram, YouTube, and the Internet. You "see" all these great lives people are living and wish you were them. I watched a documentary once on some Middle Eastern people who kept exotic cats as pets. They were riding to town in their big luxury cars, taking photos out the window with their cheetah for social media. A reporter asked one of the young men how he could afford all the animal care and the lavish lifestyle he was posting online. He admitted, "It's all fake." He said that some of the people were rich, but most of the pictures were just for show. He did not have a big cat or a big car. The car was rented, and for a fee, people let him take pictures with lions. People devote a lot of effort to keeping up an image. In the end, image doesn't even matter—substance does.

The moral of the story: Not everything is what we think it is. Don't let unsupported, emotionally charged beliefs that took root in your mind. Most of these faulty beliefs come from when we were young, impressionable, vulnerable, and immature. Don't defeat yourself before you even attempt something. Rather, call on that voice of objectivity inside your mind to help you differentiate between what is true and what is false; and when you realize that something you were holding on to is nothing but a faulty belief based on little more than subjective ego and emotion, let it go and move on toward a more realistic, balanced, forward thinking, progressive mindset.

Step #5: Avoid Negative Sources

The negative critic, as we've learned, originates from past and present negative experiences. These experiences are found in negative people, negative communications, and negative relationships. To prevent the air of negativity from surrounding you, you must avoid its sources. Words and experiences have power—their power to influence cannot be overstated. Those who have managed to gather followings in history have a particularly adept way with words. Carefully crafted words from charismatic people can charm thousands or millions of people. We've already talked about one of the most talented, persuasive orators of all time: Hitler is an extreme example of the ability to hold sway over people's minds with the written and spoken word—just look at some of his old footage for evidence, how he starts off slowly but then masterfully and convincingly rouses his audience to a point where they're overtaken by pride- and propaganda-induced emotion. And then there's also the Charles Manson and David Koresh types of this world, who are often megalomaniacs who feed their own hunger for power by preying on people's deepest insecurities and fears. On the flip side are the orators who use their talents for good: Socrates, Plato, Voltaire, MLK Jr., Mahatma Gandhi, Mandela, Abraham Lincoln, Winston Churchill. Both positive and negative influencers understand the value of words and learned how to use them to meet their aims.

It's the negative people with whom you want to avoid having relationships. There are two types of negative people I like to label the "scrapers" also known as a "hater" and the "crushers." The scrapers do not have good things to say about us, but their words hold little weight in our minds because they hold little value to us. It's like walking down a street and accidentally brushing a stranger's shoulder—when he calls you out, it hardly affects you because he means nothing to you. Or a visitor from another company in the conference room who isn't impressed by one of your comments—you just shake it off because this person doesn't even know you. These are the people whose abuses don't have the power to injure you, they only scrape the surface. At worst, you have a temporary burst of anger at them—like a driver who yells at you at the window—but once your anger is vented, you don't hold on to the incident.

Crushers, however, are negative people who are important to us by virtue of their positions in our lives: parents, children, spouses/partners, bosses, friends, coworkers, teammates, and other influential figures who hold a place in our daily lives, if not our hearts. A crusher might be a miserable mother who constantly tells you the better life she would have had were you not born. A teacher or mentor at school has the ability to crush your self-belief as well. When a scraper talks, you can easily disregard it; when a crusher criticizes, it can have devastating repercussions.

To avoid such soul-crushing people and experiences, listen to the warning bells when you think you may be entering an abusive relationship. If you enter it anyway or didn't learn the nature of the relationship until you were already in too deep, get out as soon as you can. If you can't immediately get out physically, get out mentally. Devise a plan of escape; it might take you a while to enact—you can't just run out on someone you're living with or leave your family home as a minor or quit an awful job—but with the help of friends and various sources of support (guidance counselors, pastors, therapists, other family members), you can find a way to get out from under the rubble a crusher produces. Some people become addicted to the pain and sorrow of being abused and crushed. You've heard the argument that it's better to feel something than nothing, right? That doesn't mean you have to feel something bad. You can replace numbness and apathy with good things and light, but first you have to create the space and room in your life to take more positive steps. I don't even know you, but I know you are a beautiful human being with a beautiful soul. Do not let anybody try to extinguish that. You're better than the abuse that has been handed to you! It helps to know that it's not actually about you, anyway—crushers crush because of their own discontent, their own massive insecurities, their own self-destructive tendences. They're unhappy, and they don't want to feel alone in their unhappiness. Their unfinished business is being projected onto you. You have the power of not allowing this into your life.

If your boss is a crusher, it can be extremely stressful and unfair to face that every day. So don't. Talk to HR about a transfer. Come home each evening and apply for at least one new job online per day. Plan out with your spouse how you can transition to a better position or start your own business! If your mother thinks your house is too small or your father mocks you for loving ballet, remember this: Those are only their opinions. They cannot crush your own beauty, dreams and perfection unless you allow them to keep doing so. If your own husband or wife tells you you're just average, it's just their opinion. You have to remember your boundaries of what you are going to accept and not accept from them. How to you want to be spoken to? How do you want to be treated? How do you want to be loved? You love them dearly and they're the closest person to you, but they still do not define who you are nor do they have the right to treat you as if you are a second or third-class citizen. Read some relationship-building books together, enter marriage counseling by yourself or together from a professional, seek guidance from clergy or community leaders you trust. You don't have to exit a relationship that is either essential to you or unavoidable in your life, that being said, I don't recommend anyone to say in an abusive relationship however, the choice is ultimately yours. If you want to be happy and fulfilled, you do have to change your thoughts about yourself first then the circumstances to get out from under the crusher's foot.

When at all possible, do not grant an audience to a crusher. Some people enjoy dragging other people in the mud through gossiping, spreading rumors, or using passive-aggressive behaviors to destroy another person's reputation. When the trash talk begins, do not talk back. Just get up and leave. You are better than that!

There might be people in your life who you should have let go of a long time ago. So-called friends who don't support and appreciate you but instead pretend they're just teasing you with their mockery, envy, or "helpful" advice. They'll try to taunt you with silly comments aimed at triggering your vulnerabilities. You do not have to react to these triggers. Oftentimes, you can choose to slowly withdraw from these people, so subtly they might not even realize it.

It's challenging enough in our lives to fight our own negative voices—you don't need to exacerbate this challenge by granting entrance to external negative voices that are not working to your benefit. Work to your benefit yourself by proactively disallowing space to people who strengthen the voice of your negative inner critic at the expense of your positive inner critic. When you are in an environment with constant negativity, you must find a way to escape. When you can't escape for a time, then you must find a way to tap into and connect to the positivity in that environment. You can find it, you can!

I know you can, because I did. At the age of twelve, I moved back to the town where I was born, Oroville, California, and was raised in a neighborhood filled with crime and drugs. As I walked to school, I saw people shooting up drugs in the alleys, I saw people wasting away and missing out on all the opportunities life presents. In my town, there were lots of incredible athletes who could have gone to a Division I or Division II college on a full athletic scholarship ... but most of them didn't. Many people everywhere from all walks of life find excuses for why they didn't make it: skin color, gender, disability, disadvantage. There are always going to be people and things that stand in the way of your dreams. But there are no monuments erected of people who were really good at making excuses.

Shaquem Griffin lost a hand at age four. He wanted to play football with the other kids in his community, and so that's what he set out to do—he didn't allow anyone to tell him he was incapable or label him as handicapped. It was a good, valid excuse, but he refused to adopt that excuse for himself. He was doubted in Little League, in high school, in college. He was told to abandon football, find something else that was easier. He used the negative energy of the "scrapers" and "crushers" to fuel his ambitions on the field instead, coupling it with the same ingredient you'll hear me touting over and over again: good old-fashioned hard work, dedication, and passion! When asked how he learned to catch with one hand, he simply stated, "When you get hit in the face a few times, you quickly learn." He didn't let the negative inner critic structure his life.

A coach once said, "I'll be happy if he can hit five repetitions on the bench press with his prosthetic hand." Shaquem got fired up and pushed twenty repetitions at 225 pounds with his prosthetic limb! At UCF in 2018, he ran the fastest forty-yard dash in combine history for a linebacker since 2003. He made NFL history by being the first person with one hand to be drafted into the NFL. He currently plays for the Seattle Seahawks. Shaquem Griffin is not just playing the sport he pledged to play as a kid, he's playing at the very highest level possible in the world!

Do you find yourself surrounded by negativity? Do you often come up with different excuses why you stay there? Get out your journal and write down the excuses you grant yourself to allow hangups from your past to block your purpose in life or limitations to get in the way of your dreams. Next write down what all of the "scrapers" and "crushers" have said about you and then mark an "X" through it. Reclaim the emotional *territory* that they have taken from you in your personal life. Yes, the harder the difficulties you face, the harder you'll have to work to overcome them. But this is your time to work through your limitations—this is the time to banish as much negativity from your life as you can so you can focus your attention on achieving your personal goals.

Step #6: Make Better Life Decisions

It's easy to blame other people for our misfortunes. It's easy to blame our recklessness on our childhood. Our life choices directly affect and influence our thought patterns. When you choose to be difficult, you will always have problems with people, tempers will always be lost, and hurtful things will always be said.

To be good, to be better, is a decision you can make. It's a decision to focus yourself. It's a decision to work hard. When you spend all your time lolling and have nothing to show for it, it isn't anybody else's fault. If you make bad life decisions, your lifestyle choices will be limited.

No one gets rich or poor by mistake. Sure, there's a degree of luck to our fortunes, but they depend far, far more on the decisions we make and the actions we take. People who don't make large salaries don't have to squander their paychecks on women, wine, and a good time. Unhappy, disappointed men don't have to abuse their wives, their children. When you do not respect yourself, how can you respect anybody else? If you do only what you like, when you like, and how you like, there're bound to be repercussion for that type of lifestyle.

So, choose to make better life decisions. Actively make that choice. Decide to work hard. Decide to be prudent. Decide to be patient. Save and invest some of your money. Enroll in some form of continuing education to expand your outlook and opportunities. Seek counseling help if you need it; work on changing yourself, not pressuring others to change for you.

Some people are in the wrong fields—doing the wrong things at the right time. Careers should be fulfilling and well suited to people's constitutions. When a natural people person decides to become a CPA, going against their innate grain is almost destined to create blockages. When someone who can't sit still opts to take a desk job, it just isn't going to work for long. When you're in the wrong field, you'll hear a voice in your head: *This isn't what I want. I want more than this for myself. There's something better for me out there.* This isn't necessarily the voice of negativity; it sounds like the voice of objectivity pushing you to assess your longer-term goals and start finding a way there. Similarly, when a client is disappointed in you for not completing a seven-day job after fourteen days, he isn't being negative—he's telling you like it is. Rather than lashing out at him for saying something you don't want to hear, ask yourself the more important question: Why didn't you get the job done? What about your current occupation isn't aligned with your authentic self?

If you're dishonest with people and situations around you, why are you upset with the dishonesty around you? You yourself created or at least are contributing to a dialogue of dishonesty, and you yourself can make the conscious decision to live in truth instead. The universe has a way of coming full circle. As the Apostle Paul said, "Be not deceived; God is not mocked: for whatsoever a man soweth, that shall he also reap. For he that soweth to his flesh shall of the flesh reap corruption; but he that soweth to the Spirit shall of the Spirit reap life everlasting. And let us not be weary in well doing: for in due season we shall reap, if we faint not. "Galatians 6:7-9, KJV.

When you're alone and being honest with yourself, what do you say to yourself? Some people are quick to judge and criticize themselves at the slightest presence of issues; other people are quick to point the blame elsewhere. Do you find yourself complaining to others about things that just aren't right? Do you sit down and try to find solutions to those issues, or do you run away from them? Here are some signs that you're not making good decisions for yourself: if you're notoriously inconsistent about your life goals; if others can't rely on you; if you're not considered trustworthy. It's never too late to shift your behaviors by thinking rationally about how they affect others. It's utterly manageable and doable to connect rational thought to our emotions.

Peel away the façade of subjectivity that cloaks your self-perception and aim to be objective about your strengths, challenges, and life decisions. Being positive isn't the same as fooling oneself. Self-appraisal isn't meant to bloat one's ego. If you know you are functioning beneath your full potential, admit that you know you are—and then take the necessary steps to expand your capabilities. You only have to start with the first step.

If you are good, then know you are good ... but do you want to be excellent? If you are the best, then know you are the best .... but also realize that this means other people will likely be gunning for your status or position, so you don't want to just rest on your laurels and stop striving. Even when you are at the top of your game, there is always more work to be done. Those who have climbed and have remained at the top understand this. When you heed the combined inner voice of your positivity and your objectivity, you'll make better life decisions and you'll therefore have a better and abundant life.

I have talked with many teenagers who knew they were skating by academically in school. I knew they could be better by making more of an effort in the classroom. I would see some of these kids in the principal's office. We would sit down and have a conversation about how they got there. Many times, they would come up with a reason or excuse as to why they were there: "It's not my fault," "Thomas made me do it," "The teacher doesn't like me." We began working on taking responsibility for one's own actions, the importance of respecting the space of others, and utilizing their talents and gifts. One of the highlights of my career was seeing one particular child from a poor crime infested neighborhood whose family was struggling with poverty, drug abuse, and incarceration walk across the stage to receive his diploma. His family was so proud of him, and the smile on his face when he looked over at them and raised his hands in victory was something I'll never forget.

The earlier in our lives that we start making good decisions for ourselves, the sooner we get on the track we're meant to follow. But as long as you're still here, that means you can still get on your track—or back on your track—anytime to choose to. You simply have to decide.

Nothing that you set your mind to do is impossible it maybe a struggle but not impossible! It starts with the mindset that we allow in our consciousness. It is the belief that we allow to lie within our soul or being. When fighting for the rights of enslaved Africans brought here to this country, many abolitionists were becoming discouraged and disillusioned because of the length of time and the struggle to free black people in bondage. Fredrick Douglas gave words of encouragement and said to them, "Without struggle there can be no progress." Do you give up when times get hard? Do you throw in the towel when life gives you a beating? Don't allow the inner critic to cheat you out of your reward because your dream and vision for your life is right around the corner!

Step #7: Turn Lemons into Lemonade

Do not get attached to the sourness of life, the pain of life. Everyone is allowed a mourning period when something tragic happens, but after mourning, one must heal. The mourning period is a time when you can give yourself permission to grieve. Healing is an ongoing process, one that involves development from the pain. But for some people, staying in the mourning becomes comfortable. They mourn their failed marriages; they mourn their children's bad habits; they mourn their childhood; they mourn the death of a loved one. They never stop mourning, and by doing so, they refuse to give healing a chance. At some point, we must let go and look beyond the present vista. After war comes reconciliation and rehabilitation. Unfortunately, some people's hearts are still at war years after the war has ended.

It's important to give yourself closure. If the man you love deserted you, it doesn't mean you will never find love again. You can grieve your loss for a while, but a time will come when you must heal and grow from the experience. People who don't grant themselves the chance to grow from life's tragedies don't learn how to move forward from the grieving process. They stay attached to the past—like to an ex-husband who is now happily remarried. Obsolete attachments do nothing but create more grief—you can even allow them to break your own burgeoning happiness, like a new marriage of your own.

Healing means growth, letting go, and forgiving. Turning your lemons into lemonade by turning your bitter experiences into sweet memories. Even if you were the one at fault, with time, you can do this. With time, you can forgive yourself your past misdeeds. Everyone makes mistakes, and no matter how grave, those mistakes are forgivable. If you hold on to thorns, you will bleed. Do not live all your life on thorns because of the bad things you did. However horrible your actions were, if you can find peace in forgiving yourself, there's a chance for you.

For some people, closure is impossible. A mother who loses her child might find it impossible to leave the mourning stage. If she knows the child is dead, she can mourn the child and eventually begin to heal. But some parents don't know what's become of their child. Children are kidnapped, children disappear on the streets, children are victims of sex trafficking—it happens. In such cases, closure isn't a choice of the mind, it's literally unattainable. This is a very dark and unfortunate place to be—I can hardly think of anything worse. But even in the worst of circumstances, there are strategies to cope. For such people, Freud advised *compartmentalization*. To compartmentalize one's mind is to segment thoughts and feelings into different mental divisions and partitions so that conflicting cognitions can coexist simultaneously but separately—in simplest terms, someone can hold the ability to be happy and go through the grieving process at the same time. The feeling of loss doesn't go away, it's just filed in another part of the mind so that some space can be freed for other, less upsetting, or even positive experiences. So a mother who cannot currently find closure regarding her missing child is still capable of finding happiness in her remaining children or other passions if she can process the loss of her child if she can compartmentalize in a healthy manner.

Journal in hand, exploring these painful experiences might

begin to evoke some repressed or forgotten memories that need your attention. You might begin to understand why you have carried this tremendous burden for such a long time and you are now ready to begin to put it to rest, experience a peaceful resolve, and find closure. What ways of releasing to you feel may work for you? It might be

- Creating a ritual
- A ceremony
- A collage of pictures
- Farewell celebration

Search what works for you and allow your positive and objective critic speak you as you are writing in your journal.

Bad things happen to both good and bad people. We've been reading about some of these stories in this book, like Alex Zanardi's and Shaquem Griffin's. These examples show us that even when the odds are stacked against us, when we collide with the most unfortunate of events, we can still get back up and achieve amazing feats. Napoleon Hill stated "Strength and grow come only through continues effort and struggle." When life gives us lemons, as it often does, we must turn it into lemonade with resilience and determination. We must learn to give up an injurious past for a better future.

Step #8: Celebrate Life's Small Victories and Look to Winning Bigger Battles

If we do not celebrate ourselves once in a while, we might allow negativity to rule our minds. When you achieve a small victory, you can use the victory as an impetus to take on bigger challenges. A man who is victorious as a state-level wrestling champion has the capacity to compete at the national level. If he does well nationally, perhaps he might be the next gold medalist for the Olympic Games. But it all began with local wrestling matches, most likely when he was in middle school or junior high. Most champions are not born.

Champions are made through hard work, talent, determination, and perseverance. As we have learned in this book some people had to struggle to get to their championship level. So, allow yourself to take great pride and pleasure in your small accomplishments, because they are what pave the way for larger ones.

Now, how you choose to commemorate your small victories are entirely up to you—the point is just to acknowledge them, appreciate them, and take ownership of what you have achieved for yourself through celebrations and self-care. To enjoy the ride, not just the destination. Celebrating for you might mean five minutes of mediation, taking a road trip for yourself, mountain biking, fishing, going to a concert that you always wanted to go to, giving yourself "gold stars" on a spreadsheet. What's important is that you formally recognize when you have met a life goal, or milestone, however small ... and then let out a deep breath to invite in yet another challenge!

Take care to not mourn your victories, however. Contradictory as it may seem, some people actually feel a sense of loss after they've achieved something they've been working for a long time—there's a letdown of sorts, a slowing down of the great push that's kept you going, an adrenaline crash. To avoid this, you need only look forward onto new challenges, not backward onto "finished" business. A composer who has completed a soundtrack doesn't just stop there— she needs a new project once that one's done. A novelist can't just stop after one book—he needs a new plot line in his head to keep his juices flowing and his creativity afire. A real estate agent can't just sell one house and call it day. To keep the negative critic at bay that may tell us our accomplishments are either too small or too anticlimactic once they're complete, celebrate your past, enjoy your present, and keep looking to the future. Taking on new challenges and scaling ever-greater heights is what keeps us all vibrant, vital, and victorious this is what gives energy to the positive critic.

Step #9: Learn from Your Past

Those who fail to learn from past mistakes are condemned to repeat them. We are humans after all, and to err is human. The past is meant to be forgiven, but beyond forgiveness, knowledge must come. It's one thing to let go of the past, and it's another to gain a greater understanding from it to prevent a reoccurrence of a past wrong.

After World War I, the world didn't learn. Countries reconciled and rehabilitated, but thirty years later, the world was at war again. It was only after the unprecedented devastation of whole races of people and the irrevocable dropping of not one, but two atomic bombs that the world seemed to sit back and take notice of what had really been done to the planet and to humanity. Rebuilding cities, redrawing boundaries, holding trials, making reparations, and even signing treaties isn't enough—to avoid recurrences of more wars, more drastic measures must be put in place. Prevention before there's a need for a cure. That's a good indicator of learning from the past.

Painful occurrences have happened to all of us, and sometimes we, too, have to sit back and objectively analyze the causes of those occurrences to minimize them in the future. A man who crashes his car due to reckless driving can forgive himself all he wants and even be forgiven the damage he caused, but if he doesn't accept and assimilate the knowledge that reckless driving is bad, sooner or later he'll crash another car. And next time, he or someone else might not get out alive.

We must ask the right questions about our past mistakes to uncover the learning in them. Let's say you took out a loan to start a business that folded within a year; you used your home as collateral for the loan, and now the bank is threatening to take your house. After the ordeal is over, it's not about asking your wife and children to forgive you or paying back the money your grandfather lent you to bail you out. If you want to somehow profit from the mistake by taking something valuable away from the experience, you need to take a good, hard look at where and how you went wrong so you don't retrace those steps again. Finally, we have to make the necessary actions of making things right as difficult as it can be.

People who run away from their pasts are bound to meet back up with it in their future. We must face the music to learn the tune. Sometimes we're at fault, wholly or partially, for painful episodes in our past, like the case of someone driving under the influence and injuring someone else. But sometimes we're not at fault at all, like when we're abused by an elder or neglected by a parent. Either way, if we don't find a way to glean valuable lessons from our hardships, we went through them for nothing, they were just an event and not a growth experience.

Journal in hand, exploring these embarrassing experiences might begin to evoke some repressed or forgotten memories that need your attention. You might begin to understand why you have carried this tremendous burden for such a long time and you are now ready to begin to correcting mistakes, experience a peaceful resolve, and find closure for yourself and others. What ways of correcting may work for you? It might be

- A phone call
- Setting up payments
- Returning an item that is causing friction
- Volunteer work

Step #10: Learn from Other People's Experiences

Our experiences are great resources, but we do not have to go through every negative experience life offers just because we want to learn. I love the fact that I've made some mistakes, and I love the fact that I have learned from my mistakes, but there are some mistakes I do not wish to ever make in life and some experiences I wish never to have. I have seen other people go through them, and I have seen the consequences of them in their lives. So we can learn by watching, not just by doing.

In my upbringing, I have seen the effects of drugs on neighbors and communities. In my practice, I have seen the effects of infidelity on a marriage. When I teach, I see the effects of lack of discipline and paralyzing fears on young people who don't believe in themselves. I don't need to live these experiences myself to believe in the power of what they can teach us.

Look at the lives of the people around you. You won't have to look very far to see the ramifications of both their vices and their virtues. Warren Buffet spends almost all his time studying financials and lives a very modest lifestyle. Is it any surprise that he's the "Oracle of Omaha"? Bill Clinton almost lost his presidency because of a careless, foolhardy sexual indiscretion, just as Tiger Woods almost lost his career. Both men made grave mistakes. Both men suffered for their mistakes, learned from their mistakes, and were able to slowly build themselves back up. When we look at other public or private lives, there's a treasure trove of learning material there. We don't need to have a negative occurrence ourselves to avoid the negative thought pattern and negative feedback from our inner critic that result. Be grateful for all the other people in our midst who serve as teachers in this way.

Step #11: Find Your Passion

The mind is just as vast as the universe, unbound by space and time limitations. Our existence and intelligence are based upon how much of our mind can be accessed by the brain. Interestingly, the limitations we have as humans often give us opportunities to be excellent in a few fields—if we tried to pursue them all, we could master none. Only a few individuals have been able to achieve genius in more than five fields, among them Leonardo Da Vinci, a painter, sculptor, engineer, architect, politician, physicist, builder, and more. But even Da Vinci had limitations and left behind many unfinished projects.

He may have been the rarest of geniuses, but in the end, he was still a mortal man.

The mind also has the ability to favor one field over another. In academia, one person will be drawn to literature, another to rhetoric, yet another to etymology. In science, there's incredible diversity between and among and hard sciences and the soft sciences, and certain people will excel at just one. In sports, some people run fast, jump high, throw long, swim like dolphins, or skate like ballerinas. Others will be musically inclined or adore animals or love to work with their hands or have heightened senses that lead to singular pursuits.

No matter what your particular proclivities or limitations, there's passion and purpose out there for us all. We just have to find it.

When we do, life doesn't just become easier, it becomes infinitely more interesting. When we know what we love to do, we can incorporate it into our lives as much as possible to reap the greatest possible joy and meaning from it. When we're sure of what we want to do for a living, we can draw the straightest line to that occupation, making the best use of our energy and effort. When you work in a field you love and work really hard at it, you will produce incredible results.

When you don't know where you're going, on the other hand, it's easy to lose focus. To waste time, to squander and wander, to be disappointed in yourself and your life, and to feel disengaged from the business of living. Because the negative critic feeds on negative experiences, working in a field you are not passionate about supplies the inner critic with a narrative whereby it critically judges you When a person isn't passionate about what they do, failure becomes a friend. It's difficult to be persistent in the wrong field. It's difficult to excel in the wrong line of work. Persistence alone doesn't guarantee success: An untalented professional will be as good as a talented amateur; it's the talented professional that hits the jackpot.

So, if there's one piece of advice I'd give anyone trying to turn away from negative forces or influences in their life and toward a more fulfilling, productive, and proactive existence, it would be to find your passion. Those who do so early in life are very lucky. Especially if what they love and what they're good at turns into something financially and professionally rewarding.

Are you unsure about what path to take in your life or career? What thoughts motivate you to get out of bed in the morning? When you go to bed, what do you dream about? What activities put a smile on your face? If you're already on the path of your calling, staying there and progressing onward is a surefire way to quell your negative inner critic and let your positive inner critic reign supreme. For you will have meaning, value, purpose, and intention in your life. Those are invaluable—those will get your through anything. If you haven't yet determined what ignites you, then now is the time to go on a hunt for it, so you can ensnare it, hold it close, and let it enrich the rest of your days. Here are some tips on how to zero in on your passion:

1. **Find your interests:** Look for the things that interest you. You might have just a few, you might have many. List your interests in your journal and then put a star by the three that appeal to you the most. If the three are related (for example, song lyrics, poetry, and plays), then try to identify the common denominator, which here seems to be writing. That might be your primary passion. If the interests are unrelated (for example, yoga, acting, and drumming), identify the one you do with the most ease.

2. **Find your spark:** Related to but different from your common denominator is the prize you can't take your eyes off of. Okay, so you've pinpointed the written word as your dominant interest, but boy do you want to be a music star! You're fascinated by the life of a musician; the first time you visited a studio, you felt intense happiness, like you were home; and in your spare time, you prefer to listen to rap music. Your spark therefore might just be writing and recording rap music. Or maybe your interests are gardening, foreign cuisine, and creating processes—your calling might just be as a cookbook author or chef.

3. **Be diligent:** Even if you haven't yet found your passion, spark, or calling, it doesn't give you the right to live below the level of excellence. To be lazy or settle for a subpar existence. Sticking with the examples above, let's say you just finished school and don't know how to set about becoming a rapper. Call on your voice of objectivity to devise the next logical steps you can follow to diligently pursue your dream. Immerse yourself in the genre by playing rap music night and day and taking notes on what you discover about its structure and presentation. Contact leaders in the industry to ask for training or internships. Approach musical groups to pitch writing lyrics for them. Start your own group. Take a music appreciation course, a modern poetry course. Read stories and biographies of successful rappers. Perform at open mic nights or in poetry slams. Most of all: write, write, write, then record and post your own creations. We don't all realize our dreams and even hard work sometimes doesn't pay off like we imagined, but I'd be willing to bet that if you take your commitment to your passion seriously, you'll start seeing some serious results!

Journal Exercise: Name just one passion you want to feature more in your life right now. Now name three to five manageable, doable steps you can start taking today to follow that passion more than you have been.

Step #12: Elevate Others

The call to elevate others isn't a call to change the world. It's not a huge moral burden. If you have ever been the victim of constant word thrashing, you will understand that it is better to keep quiet than to say things that will unnecessarily hurt another human being.

Most times, the hunter is the hunted; the abuser is the abused.

When you live a life that constantly tries to rub one person in the mud, you will eventually land in the mud. Hatred and bitterness are often paid back in kind. A horrible person will face grave adversity—even in their own household.

Do not be someone who puts people down just because you can, just because you were put down, or just because you feel you are better or more talented than them. You might be the president of a Fortune 500 company, but it doesn't make you superior to the lady who serves you coffee at your favorite coffee shop. When you attain a position of power, influence, or authority, your words carry more weight than usual. It is important to be a good steward of your power. You must not throw negative words around. Doing so shows an utter abuse of the position to which you've been elevated.

Elevate people within your immediate environment, including your family members. No matter what you become, you will still go home to them, and if you sow so much negativity on your way out, you will reap as much negativity on your way in. A lot of children have been socially affected because their fathers failed to praise them or their mothers were balls of constant criticism. Recall the power of words, and don't add more negative words to your life by uttering them yourself. Even jokingly, refrain from putting people down. Sarcasm might seem funny to you, but it's a sneaky way of communicating anger, resentment, insecurity, and self-doubt. When people around you are down, you will trip on them and crash; but if you elevate the people around you, they will pick you up when you fall.

This world has seen the level of violence and injustice that can be generated when amoral people are lifted to positions of influence and power. Tyrants, bullies, and cowards have used religion, race, language, geography, culture, and myriad other differences as flimsy excuses to oppress and deny others. Don't contribute even one iota to that cesspool. Rise above it by raising yourself and others. The world needs a lot of healing, and it will heal faster with one less negative person. Be a good person who positively imparts goodness on people. It will come back to you a hundredfold!

Step #13: Build Positive Relationships

When we are young, we are limited by choice as to the longevity and quality of our relationships. As we grow older, the limitations narrow, and we have more freedom to choose our friends and acquaintances. Good relationships exhibit good communication, experiences, support, and growth. Bad relationships do the opposite. As the sayings go, birds of a feather flock together, and if you sleep with dogs, you will rise with fleas.

The people you walk with influence you in ways you might not even realize. Their attitudes flow into your consciousness and subconsciousness to such a degree that even in their absence, you might begin to act out their principles and values. So as you mature and carve out your own path, you must be careful about those you let into your circle. An honest man and a thief will make an honest thief—all the more crooked, all the less truthful.

The first set of vices a teenager will be introduced to will often come from their peers. Most teenagers start drinking alcohol because they have friends who drink. Most teenagers who steal have friends who steal. They are influenced by their peers, and they begin to duplicate the attitudes of their peers. Some join gangs because somebody told them it was the "in" thing or they were looking for a place of belonging. Some begin doing drugs to prove a point—that they want to get back at someone or run away from something.

The saddest part is that none of these attempts to fit in or stand out get people anywhere. In worst-case scenarios, youngsters don't even live long enough to later understand the errors of their ways. When we're surrounded by negative relationships, the negative critic will tell us that approval and acceptance can be found in these self-defeating behaviors. But nothing could be farther from the truth. The truth is—for all of us: rich and poor, old and young, blessed or unfortunate—approval, acceptance, and self-love are actually found when we surround ourselves with positive relationships infused with these characteristics:

- **Honesty:** A relationship must be built on trust and honesty. A relationship is healthy when both parties can be open about each other's weaknesses. A friend or a lover who feels you are too competitive should be able to tell you that (directly or indirectly, depending on your personality). When you are surrounded by people who don't tell you the truth or people who tell you only what you want to hear, you're in superficial and selfish relationships. Sometimes, one or both of the parties is engaged in this kind of relationship because they're profiting off it somehow—maybe from the adulation received for a talent or skill or financial benefits. Be on the lookout for people who like you because of what you have or what you've become, not because of who you are.

- **Positivity:** This is an important factor in any good relationship. Any relationship that radiates negativity is a bad relationship and must be avoided or abandoned. If a person close to you constantly has negative things to say to you and about you, they are fueling the negative critic that already exists within you. In the union between the external and the internal negative critic, you are giving yourself over to be defeated. Some people constructively make observations about you as a person; these people truly care about your growth and are not afraid to speak up when they know you need to hear something. Constructive criticism takes away power from the negative inner critic, allowing us to make better choices for ourselves.

- **Growth:** A relationship should promote personal and professional growth. If your friends think, talk, and do the same things they did five years ago, then they are not growing. At some point, you might find that you have completely outgrown some of the people in your life. When a new bride is focused on building a home and starting a family with her husband, she'll outgrow the friends who are still dating multiple people at the same time and spending their nights partying. When one of two buddies who got hired at a startup job together moves on to a great promotion and greater goals for himself while the other is content to just languish where he is, the relationship probably won't last much longer. And if you take up a deep interest in something new, like hiking or travel it will be far better for your relationship if your partner wants to share your interest or at least support it.

Step #14: Understand the Self

"Man, know thyself" are arguably the three most essential words ever spoken by philosophy. Attributed to Socrates, this maxim assumes that the inner workings of each person are different and that it is incumbent upon each person to take the time to understand themselves.

We are all uniquely created. We have individual combinations of talents, interests, weaknesses, strengths, personality traits, and inherent qualities, along with varying thought, belief, and behavior patterns. This is why two people who grow up in exactly the same circumstances will not become the same type of person. Scientifically, two people cannot have the same fingerprints; even identical twins have differing DNA.

Understanding the self, *your* self, is crucial for defeating the negative inner critic. Why do certain things get to you, make you so angry? Do you have resentment for someone in your life despite the seemingly good relationship you appear to have on the outside? When do you feel most authentic? Inauthentic? What is standing in the way of you pursuing your best life? Questions like these spark long inner conversations and can reveal certain truths about our lives. If we're willing to look deep within, we can begin to see ourselves from different perspectives, all our multifaceted angles.

Acceptance is a process of the mind, and people must learn to accept themselves if they truly want to become better versions of themselves. You can't accept who you are until you know who you are, and that's why self-concept, self-confidence, self-esteem requires coming to terms with your inner truths. When you lift the veil that covers and protects your innermost self, the truths that emerge can be a bitter pill, hard to swallow. Some of them, at least. But freedom exists within the truth as well—freedom to forgive, to heal, and to hope. That's what lies on the other side of understanding yourself: forgiveness, healing, and hope.

Growth is the end result. When we objectively assess our lives, tackle our issues, and attempt to remedy our deficits, we will grow. Growth, too, is a process and it might take some time, but you can eventually mature to a level where you've diminished the negative critic holding you back from the higher self that wants you to soar.

Step #15: Be Relentless and Hopeful

One thing the negative inner critic tries to take away from you is the feeling of hope. When you feel all hope is lost, you lose your will to fight. When you lose your will, you miss out on the abundance that life has to offer you. If you are being bombarded with voices that tell you that you can never be free, it is on you to prove those voices wrong. You must rise up against the force trying to defeat you and do the direct opposite, become the opposite.

The negative inner critic can be relentless, especially when it comes from repressed experiences. This type of voice won't go away easily. The battle against the self can be fierce, and if you give up too easily or too soon, you might not be able to turn your life around. You must keep on fighting. Fighting for yourself.

Because you are relentless too. And the whole of you is stronger than the part of you in which the negative critic resides. It cannot be overstated about the value of: Hard work. Diligence. Perseverance.

Relentless determination. With these weapons, you can tame your inner demons, apply your hard-won life lessons, and redirect the language and processes of your negative inner critic toward a life filled with hope and achievement of your goals.

CHAPTER 7

Building the Voice of Positivity

Champions aren't made in gyms. Champions are made from something they have deep inside them—a desire, a dream, a vision. They have to have the skill and the will. But the will must be stronger than the skill.

—Muhammad Ali

The last chapter talked about combating the voice of negativity. When negativity is diminished, there's more room in your mind and in your life for other things—but you don't want those other things to be meaningless or hedonistic, to be short-sighted or short-term strategies that won't actually advance you along your chosen path, or, worst of all, to be new negative thought patterns or behaviors that simply replace the old banished ones. For example, if you're able to successfully remove yourself from a friendship you've long outgrown that was bringing little more than toxicity and anxiety to your life, it does you no good to fill the void with replacement mental messages that are still damaging and self-defeating: *Yeah, Justine's constant criticism is gone, but now what am I left with? Nothing—not one close friend to confide in or go out with. A bad friend is better than no friend at all. Oh my God, what have I done? I'll never find somebody new who gets me like she did.*

It's quite common and easy to fall into this type of mental trap or pattern: Finally leaving the daily misery of a bad marriage only to start a new life filled with daily fears, doubts, and insecurities. Giving up a smoking addiction, but replacing it with a food addiction. Real, lasting progress hasn't been made here; one negative tape has simply been swapped out with another negative tape that will repeatedly play in the mind.

But there's an antidote to slipping into the pattern of the comfort of negativity. In weakening your areas of weakness, you want to concurrently give power to your areas of strength; in other words, as hard as you work to diminish the negative voice is as hard as you should work to strengthen the positive voice. This chapter explores just that—how to not just fill the void left by departing negativity with positivity, but how to actively enhance the positive voice so that it takes up more room in your headspace.

Clearing space in your mind for positive, healthy, and fulfilling new neural pathways to take shape and take root isn't just desirable, it can be absolutely necessary to our mental well-being. This point can most clearly be seen in the case of servicemen and servicewomen who return home from various types of battlefields. The whole time they're deployed, they're desperately missing their loved ones, counting down the days of their tours of duty, praying to make it out safe and sound. But when they get home, many of them—far, far too many of them— become entrenched in a new type of suffering from post-traumatic stress disorders: trauma-induced triggers, stressors, memories, and behaviors that hold them captive even as they're now supposedly "free" from war. However, the war is still raging in the mind. They can't empty their minds of pain and suffering, and even when and if they temporarily can, the sense of sadness, despair, isolation, disinterest, and detachment might only be replaced by equally detrimental anger, hostility, aggression, and violent tendencies. Escaping the original source of the negative influences is no guarantee of an end to the negative influences.

Positivity doesn't just sprout up all by itself. Often, active intervention is needed. In the case of military veterans and survivors of trauma, intervention is usually multidimensional: varying combinations of professional counseling, skills training, coping strategies, psychological therapeutics, and more. Most beneficial of all, however, is group support—the empathy, camaraderie, and bonding that's experienced by being surrounded by those who care and truly understand what someone is going through can mean all the difference between barely living and fully living.

Fortunately, we don't have to be victims of trauma to benefit from these same approaches. Regular civilians and people from all walks of life, with all kinds of backgrounds and histories, can engage in interventions of their own making to increase the positive aspects of their mental health while they decrease the negative aspects. Your intervention might include professional therapy or a support group or educational courses or a spiritual quest. Whatever measures you choose to take, being surrounded by loving, supportive family and friends is key as you work toward the end goal of replacing failure with success, supplanting negativity with positivity, and then bolstering that positivity as much as you possibly can to solidify lasting, meaningful improvements in your life. Here are some steps to get you started on your own.

Accept Who You Are

You will never find inner freedom, mental liberation, until you accept yourself. Flaws and all. However, petulant, irresponsible, or contentious you may be, you will not achieve personal growth until you accept yourself as you are. Accept the truths of yourself. You have the power to change things about yourself that you want to change, but not until you recognize and then accept those things first.

Acceptance means understanding your uniqueness—your pet peeves, your need to straighten the pillows just so, your obsession with Egyptian history, your aversion to spicy foods, your frugality, your intolerance of dishonesty of any kind, your required dose of laughter each day, your jealousy of your brother—and then *valuing* all those things that go into your uniqueness. For there is value in any truth. And there is pride in any ownership. However grave the mistake, when you own it and make it yours, then the power to forgive yourself is yours as well. However heavy the sin you're bearing, when you recognize it, you can make the choice of doing something about it. However slowly you're progressing in your life, when you accept your own pace, you can keep moving on. Acceptance goes below the surface of just assessing your strengths and weaknesses to seek out a deep understanding of your deepest self. These are the dark places that we might be afraid of. It is when we dare to venture down the dark corridors that we will discover a part of ourselves that have been the motivating factor to why we feel the way that we feel, make the choices that we have made, and how we truly feel about ourselves. The negative critic does not like the light to shine on this part of our inner self because this is the step towards true freedom and deliverance.

As we peer into our inner self, we will discover that we are indeed much like an iceberg from the coldest parts of the earth. When you are looking at an iceberg from the boat of your ship how much of the iceberg do you see? The answer that I usually get is between 5-10%. Typically, we are looking at the top 10% percent of the iceberg. The is very reminiscent to our behavior and our emotional self. Emotions such as anger, irritation, frustration, hostility and the like are the top 10% of the iceberg. These emotions sit just above the surface. What do you think is driving these emotions? What is fueling the anger, irritation, frustration or hostility? Why do these emotions come up for you so often, especially in heated arguments with your significant other, certain family members, or on the job for instance? When you are triggered do you retreat into your mancave or isolate yourself? Do you explode? Are you passive aggressive? Do you use sarcasm as a tool? Do you see yourself using manipulative behaviors? You may think that it is your partner's actions, your job not giving you the recognition that you believe you deserve, or a boss that you feel is taking advantage of you or treating you unfairly. These emotions are usually expressed when we are feeling like we are not being heard, valued, acknowledged or recognized. You are frustrated because you feel like you are invisible or that your hard work and dedication is not being acknowledged. This negative inner conflict does not want you to have a clear understanding to the real source of surface level emotions or feelings. There is a deeper force that is underneath surface. As we take a closer look, we will discover that there is another hidden 90% of the iceberg of the self. This 90% of the iceberg has been underwater for thousands and thousands of years. Some of the edges are razor sharp to the touch! The 90% is another part of you!

The 90% is what we don't see. It is hidden from other people and very often from ourselves. Underneath the surface of the ocean water, as we venture deeper down to investigate the iceberg, we will find old remnants of unfinished business; such as resentment, not feeling good enough, uncertainty, the fear of abandonment, insecurity, the fear of attaching to others, the avoidance or fear of being vulnerable. My question to you is what is your 90%? What do you believe is driving the anger or resentment within you? This is the unfinished business that I discussed with you previously in this book. It is the voice of our fathers, the look of distain and disappointment from our caregivers, it's that one word that never left you as a child. This is the lair of the negative inner critic. We have to remember that it was not the 10% of the iceberg that sunk the Titanic it was the 90% underneath the surface!

Journal time

Journal in hand, time to begin exploring your iceberg! Write down some experiences that might begin to evoke some repressed or forgotten memories that need your attention. You might begin to understand why you have carried this tremendous burden for such a long time and you are now ready to start investigating the fissures, cracks, contours of deep-seated issues related to your iceberg. As difficult as it may seem, this is the part of your journey towards your peaceful resolve; to begin finding closure for yourself. Write down some of your 90% of the iceberg.

- Past hurts
- Family Secretes
- The word that never left your memory
- Unfinished business that you inherited from your parents
- Soul wounding

Each individual is the same in the fact that we're all different, and we must accept these differences if we want to make the best use of them in our life goals. We, too, cannot be all things to all people; we must set our sights on what we want out of life and then pursue that mission statement in our own unique way with the particular skill set we have. We must play our own game if we wish to become the master of it. search yourself to find the source of the obstacles blocking your way. Are you still hurt by the fact that your mother shows more attention to your younger sister? Do you secretly wish you were an only child? Do you fear that, deep down, you detest your father for his alcoholism and the pain it brought upon your family? Do you resent a lost childhood because you had to go out and work to help pay the bills? We may not be able to get over some of the hardships of our earlier lives, but we can get around them, see around them, if we accept that our story is our story, take ownership of that story, and find value in that story. Acceptance is the path to happiness. Happiness is a process. And a process takes time and effort.

There can be no redemption without acceptance, either. Let's say you were very hard on your child, even verbally abusive at times. You weren't aware of it at the time—not really, anyway, you didn't set out to be a father who made his child feel like a failure—but now he's a young man and your relationship is very strained. He's not the only one—you've discovered there are other people in your life who you've offended without realizing you were doing it. You don't know why. You want to know why. So you decide to get to the bottom of things. You start taking a good, hard look at your own life—hopefully, with the help of a professional who can facilitate your road to discovery—and you can now see, from your more mature vantage point, that you were just re-creating your own childhood home in your adult home. Your father was very hard on you, too; he talked to you in any tone he wanted and wasn't going to take any disrespect in return. But that was just how it was in your day—that was the accepted norm in your culture, the standards of the time and place you were raised. You didn't give much thought to your upbringing once you moved out and moved on and started a family of your own. You're a grown man now, and so is your son, but he's angry at you—he doesn't trust you and he doesn't know how to forgive you. Even with your newfound calmness, caring, and regret, your past is haunting you and your negative critic is telling you that you can't heal your relationship with your son, you can't undo what was done.

You *can* accept the truth of the situation now—an acceptance based on understanding you actively sought out—and you can act on that truth with your boy. You can do now with him and for him what you wish your own father would do with and for you to make things better concerning your past. You have a particular understanding of your son's perspective because you've lived it yourself, and you can put that shared understanding to work for you to better your relationship *now*.

We all have inner battles like this, chains we need to break through. Some are bound by the tentacles of anger. Some are drowning in their own resentment. Some are dependent on substances to hide the truth of themselves from themselves. But the earlier we're aware of our Achilles' heels, the earlier we can seek the proper help to address them and the better it will be. If you understand early enough that you are prone to alcoholism—accept that about yourself—then you can take active steps in your daily life to win that battle before it even starts, like keeping a dry house, avoiding friends and functions that involve drinking, bringing along your own beverages to social events, having a "sober buddy" to help hold you accountable.

When self-understanding leads to self-acceptance, you will more easily notice pitfalls and thus avoid them more easily. If you know you are temperamental in nature, you can establish a safe word or gesture with significant others in your life that signals it's time to walk away from an argument before it gets too intense. If you've come to accept that you're a timid individual who just won't speak up in meetings, you can put your ideas and thoughts in memos and emails instead—you still get to have your say, but in a way that's true to you.

Acceptance isn't only about allowing ourselves our negative habits and weaknesses, however. It's also about embracing our positives. You are beautifully, wonderfully, and graciously made. You are a winner and you were meant to be here. I believe that each one of us truly is a "miracle"—I don't care how trite or clichéd that sounds, there's no denying how marvelously, gloriously, and intricately a human being is wired. If you can accept the simple fact of the miracle of life, you can stop hating your body because you are, think or believe that your ugly, bald, too short, too tall, handicapped, or disabled. You can tame the negative inner critic that wants to magnify your uniqueness by criticizing your body image when you look in the mirror. You are exactly as you were meant to be, and you are beautiful.

Acceptance of our strengths is essential in life—even more essential than acceptance of our imperfections. When you accept, invite, and embrace your talents, you will find the right occupation to which to dedicate your professional life. When you know you're better suited to be a marketer or a salesperson or an electrician or a textile designer, you can go shopping for the exact right suit to wear. When you know what you do with ease and then do it, your life will be easier. The journey toward acceptance begins with the keen study of self-knowledge and then continues on into lifelong self-growth and development.

Action Tips to Promote Self-Acceptance

1. Take time to study yourself. Study your past, study your present, know your strengths, and know your weaknesses.
2. Seek help. Decide to seek help if you need it. Do not suffer in silence. If you really want to be fit and healthy but don't know how to get there on your own, you'd go to a trainer at a gym or a nutritionist. The same applies to your mental health— if your pain and struggles are beyond your own ability to remedy them with your natural strengths, seek professional or nonprofessional help. Talk to somebody. There is no shame or weakness in getting help; humans are social creatures meant to help and support each other through life.
3. Focus on your assets rather than your deficits. No one is perfect—physically or otherwise. Choose to shine a light on your beauty, intelligence, creativity, and goodness. Work them into your morning mantras. Start treating yourself better today. Start loving yourself more today.
4. Make a promise to yourself to never give up. When you fall a hundred times, get up a hundred times. Understanding and accepting the self takes time and effort. Put in the time and the effort.

Create a Life Vision and Goals

The next thing you can do for yourself to bolster the inner critic's positive aspect is to get clear on a vision for your life and then chart out goals and plans to realize that vision. This is a large undertaking, so let's break it down into multiple processes.

Set a Vision

When I think of creating a vision, my mind turns to a passage in the Bible that I use to read as a child in Sunday School class. I never understood it until I became older, (John 8) where Jesus is being questioned as to why his account of things is to be believed or trusted as true. He answers, "Even if I testify about myself, my testimony is valid, because *I know where I came from* and *where I am going.*"

I like this line here, because although "vision" can be a hard concept to capture due to the word's intrinsic elusiveness, it lies somewhere between the bookends of where you started from and where you'll end up. For some, a vision can be equated with a long-term agenda, if you will—what they set their sights on from the big-picture point of view: their own city on the hill, pot of gold at the end of the rainbow, or lighthouse steadily blinking on a jetty. Some people create actual vision boards with pictures of what they want to achieve, words that influence them, images of things they want to acquire or master. For others, a vision is more of a feeling than a construction—a sense of assurance they feel that they know what path to follow. Whatever one's sense of "vision," it is derived from will and passion. It doesn't need to be a crystal-clear picture, but it does need to light your way to where you're going.

To my mind, there are two types of vision: timed and untimed. Timed visions have a life span of at least five years, and the vision bearer (the person who has the vision) has a good degree of assurance that the vision can be realistically manifested. A high school student listened to Dr. Ben Carson's speech about his successful operation separating the heads of conjoined twins and decided right then and there that he wanted to become a neurosurgeon too. If he put in the work and studied hard, he knew he could achieve his dream, and so he started in on the schedule he'd need to follow to get there: how many years of pre-med, med school, internship, and residency. He researched the factors required and set about putting them in place as well.

Untimed visions, on the other hand, don't carry built-in assurances of being realized. The vision is clearly in focus—Kadesha *knows* she wants to be a movie animator for a big-time studio—but there are too many factors beyond the vision bearer's control for success to be reasonably assured. Kadesha has proven artistic acumen and she's got a portfolio of impressive work, but there are a lot of animators out there just as talented as she is. She can stick to it day in and day out, she can hope and she can pray, she can make as many industry connections as she can, but there's no guarantee she'll ever get hired by Hollywood. Her vision is one that might take three, ten, or twenty years to become a reality, if ever. Then again, she could get her big break next week after a video she posted on TikTok goes viral and a head honcho takes notice. Luck, not just hard work and dedication, plays a role in untimed visions.

Let's circle back to this idea of how many factors are within the vision bearer's control. Sometimes the vision bearer has virtually full control: A young woman attending a vocational program to become an electrician *will* be qualified to be an electrician at the end of all her coursework. If she passes her licensing exam, she *will* obtain her license and will then almost certainly find work as the licensed electrician she now is.

Visions that are somewhat or significantly beyond the vision bearer's control are far more difficult to achieve. A high school sophomore very much wants to spend several semesters abroad as a foreign exchange student in his upper-class years to launch his dream of becoming an international diplomat. But if his family simply cannot afford to make this happen, or if a host family cannot be found or falls through, or if a scholarship is not won to pay for living expenses overseas, it's makes the vision more difficult to come to fruition. Later on, in his life, this young man might indeed find a way to travel to his chosen destinations, but right now, the means are seem to be out his reach. Through perseverance he can find a way. He learned this through living in poverty all his life. He seen what a little can do and how his mother kept going despite not having enough, being turned away, being told "no" and shunned because of the food stamps she had to use at the checkout stand. He remembers the look on the faces of the people behind his mother as the bagger was bagging her groceries. He remembers the weight of shame and the sting of poverty in his gut. He won't let his dream and vision for his life die because he seen the perseverance of his mother and he probably can still hear the words of Jesus ringing true in his ears, *"because I know where I came from and where I am going."* His determination gives rise to the hope that is within him to keep pressing forward despite the odds. Are you willing to persevere through hard times?

A vision at the far end of either side of the spectrum sounds an alarm bell. When a vision is completely obtainable and fully within one's control, that person might not be dreaming big enough—the vision might be too comfortable. When a vision is basically unobtainable and outside one's control, the dream is likely too big, not at all realistic, like hitting the lottery to buy an island or becoming a famous movie star without ever attending acting school. But for any vision bearer, the real test of the person's attachment to the vision will come when they are faced with obstacles that threaten to derail them: Will they manage to overcome them or be engulfed by them? When someone's vision is challenged by naysayers, critics, finances, disappointments, and abandonment by people they thought would be there till the end, a lot of people give up—they give in to the fears and doubts the negative critic whispers over and over.

Great people are always faced with great odds. Always. Great dreams do not materialize easily. They take time, effort, hard work, planning, productivity, luck, and dozens of other factors. To improve the probability of *your* vision coming to pass, divide it into discrete goals.

Set Goals and Make a Plan to Achieve Those Goals

There's an old saying that goes, "Failing to plan is planning to fail." The originator of these words is debatable, but what is unquestionable is the wisdom of them. Not having a plan in place is a surefire way to lose your place along the road to your vision.

Goals are timed plans that support visions. For a vision to be effectively pursued, it must be broken into daily, short-term, and long-term goals that are enacted by actionable plans. For example, if a CEO aims to increase the net worth of his company by $500 million in ten years, his business plan can include yearly targets that increase net worth by $50 million annually. Not all plans have to be divided into equally timed goals, of course, but it is important to emphasize the step-by-step nature of a plan and its cumulative results over time. If someone's dream is to become a competitive gymnast, there is absolutely a plan that can be mapped out for which actions need to be taken, in what order, how often, and for how long. A coach will no doubt be brought in to help further refine the plan. And if turns out that only the horse and the uneven bars are areas of true potential, not the balance beam and the floor, then the plan will be adjusted to concentrate on only those two events.

Goals follow plans, and plans are the means by which vision bearers achieve their visions. They should be clear and firm and manageable. That said, it is imperative that plans are also able to evolve with changing times and circumstances, for you're sure to encounter unexpected occurrences in the enactment of *any* kind of plan. Still, that will not affect the overall trajectory of the end goal—that stays the same. Divorce is an example of something that no one ever plans to happen, but it does. The dissolution of a marriage will surely alter timing, finances, locations, family member roles and dynamics, but the spouses' dreams and visions for themselves, for their lives, will emerge intact, they'll survive the end of the marriage, even though they may have to be rerouted, delayed, or revised. Learning to adapt, evolve, survive, and thrive in new situations is simply part of the human experience—you're not going to be able to realize your vision without encountering at least some of these challenges along the way.

When you inevitably do, your clear and firm vision for yourself must overpower, gain dominion over, the negative inner critic's temptations to lead the mind to ruminations on failure, to quitting. Your will can take precedence over your doubts by setting goals—daily, weekly, monthly, yearly—that keep you organized and on point as you set about attaining them and that afford you a sense of fulfillment when you achieve them.

Easier said than done, I realize. When it comes to my own goal-setting and plan-making, organization proved to be my sore spot. I couldn't quite pinpoint why or when this belief took hold in me, but my negative inner critic repeatedly told me that I was just a disorganized person and I'd accepted that about myself for I don't know how long. It was a belief that led to anxiety. I doubted that I'd have the organizational proficiency to make it to the finish line of my goals, and this doubt spiraled into insecurities that stymied my progress.

So I decided to make conquering disorganization a goal in itself. I started by reframing my thought process and language around the whole issue: Organization—a skill, an ability that exists outside my own body, was the problem; *I* was not the problem. My name was not "Disorganization," it was not a label stamped on my head; rather, improving my organizational skills was a competency I could cultivate, an issue that *could* be resolved. Seen from this perspective (which, by the way, was not a fabrication of my own making but a more realistic way of looking at the situation—hello, voice of objectivity), the anxious feelings attached to this challenge started dissipating and I replaced them with actionable steps to achieve my goal of becoming more organized.

I placed a seashell on my end table to hold my keys, for example, so that I wouldn't keep misplacing them. I learned how to use my computerized calendar to make appointments and send me reminders. I created a filing system for all the different stacks of papers on my desk so that I could more easily locate what I needed when I needed it. Now my positive inner critic praises me when I get out the door on time and when I'm poised and ready for my next video call. That inner praise reinforces my newfound behaviors, so that I continue to replace habits of disorganization with habits of organization. I still have a ways to go in my goal, but the plan I put in place and continue to enact assures me that I will get to my intended destination with far less frustration and far more success.

Make Your Goals and Plans Concrete

Goals and plans alone are insufficient; to actually realize them, you need to make them concrete. As concrete as possible, actually.

It's not enough to say, "My goal is to be rich." "I have a vision of starting a company." "My biggest dream is to be famous." Or "All I really want for myself is to live a happy life." Each statement in and of itself is fine, but each is too vague and general to get you "where you came from to where you are going." A vision without a concrete plan is a daydream. A goal without a concrete plan is just a wish. How are you going to make it happen? What preparatory measures must you put in place? What specific steps to follow? What timeline do you need to stick to? What will you need to buy, borrow, learn, or secure? What contingencies should you put in place for when you hit detours and pitfalls? On your own or with the help of a trusted advisor, do a serious inventory of the situation and devise a definitive plan no less serious and deliberate than a business proposal must be.

In the corporate world, a businesswoman doesn't just walk into a conference room and ask for capital to invest in her idea. Long before the presentation meeting, there are months, if not years, of marketing research to conduct, spreadsheets to create, prototypes to order, test runs to do, expenses and interest rates and sales projections and profit margins to consider. And lots more! Have you ever watched an episode of *Shark Tank*? Each person who walks through those doors to pitch to the panel has a dream that they turned into a vision that they translated into a precise plan broken down into itemized goals. And they sure didn't do it over a weekend!

The point is, it's foolhardy to follow a dream blindly. "I want to be a country singer, so I'm just going to move to Nashville and see how the chips fall." Once in a blue moon, that kind of wishful thinking might pay off, but if you're serious about wanting to break through barriers and make progress in your life, better to map out an actual, tangible plan and then follow it to a T. Unplanned plans can lead to unfortunate ends. A sailor would never go on a voyage without plotting his course. A dressmaker would never just cut into fabric without outlining the pattern. And a builder would never just start hammering away without an architectural blueprint.

What goals do you currently want to set for yourself? Do you want to accomplish them in a month? A year? Five years? Pick the goal, settle on a time span in which to realistically achieve it, then devise a way to measure your productivity across that span. Let's take a simple example: "I want to read thirty books." Sounds pretty specific, but it's not. Better: "I want to start and finish thirty books in the next year, starting from today's date." From there, you can do the math—you're going to have to read at least two books for each of the twelve months, and to make up for the half dozen shortfall, you'll have to work in a third book every other month. Knowing this, perhaps you'll choose two novels per month and a shorter, nonfiction book for the alternating months. Next, start a checklist of the books you know you want to read—which ones you already have, which ones you'll get later, from a friend, a bookstore, the library. You might even want to "schedule" them at this point based on length or genre or some other parameter. As for a way to measure your progress, you can simply check off the box next to each title when you complete it, so you can track how well you're sticking to your plan.

Recall what we said about the necessity of flexibility in even the best-laid plans, however. Many things can happen over the course of a year that cause you to fall behind on your goal—an increase in work, a visiting relative, a new baby. When you're on vacation, you might find that you get through two books in two weeks. If you're committed to reading *War and Peace*, you might find that you can't even get through one in a month. So allow yourself some wiggle room and adaptability in any plan you create, so you can speed up, slow down, or "make edits" as called for. If *War and Peace* is more important to you than your set number, maybe you'll just choose to amend your goal to "more than twenty books this year." You're the goal-setter and the plan-maker, so you have the power to make adjustments that work best with the realities of your daily life.

Even as the plan-maker, though, you can't always *make* something happen. You might set a goal to get married in the next year, but if you don't even have a boyfriend or girlfriend yet, no amount of planning and mapping and charting can force true love to enter your life in the time span you desire. Similarly, you may be completely in control of a dream of yours and totally on track to achieve it when something entirely external and unexpected happens. I'm thinking of a student I once knew who was all set to graduate from college and start graduate school when his father died abruptly. Obviously, his education plans didn't factor in the untimely passing of his father, but once this calamity befell his family, he really had no other choice than to put off his plans to help his mother settle his father's affairs and reconfigure the family business.

To summarize: As regards the goals and plans you set to increase the amount of positivity in your life, factors and circumstances can arise that might require edits to your plans. Expect that—plan to have to adjust your plan at times. Depending on the magnitude of your goals, you'll likely come up against obstacles. Things don't go smoothly all the time. Sometimes things go full-on catastrophic. When faced with such odds, most people just fold—they pack up and drop out. Don't be one of those people who are only committed to their goals when the odds are on their side. Be the exceptional, extraordinary person you are by carrying on and continuing to try even when things go wrong. Especially when things go wrong.

Building the positivity in your world is like having a savings account: The more you have banked, the more you can draw on your balance when things get rocky. So hope for the best, yes, but also prepare for the unexpected. Winds will change direction, waves will ebb and flow, but the more you turn your back on the negative inner critic on the shore and look out over the horizon of the objective, the realistic, and the positive, the better you will be able to weather life's storms—armed with a plan born of your will, your tenacity, your ingenuity, your resilience, and your actions.

Action Tips to Setting Concrete Goals

1. Set a vision for the next five years of your life. Give serious thought to where you want to be living, what work you want to be doing, what pastimes you want to be engaged in in your free time. What do your days and nights look like? Who and what are you surrounded by? How are you feeling about yourself and your progress in overcoming your internal struggles? What have you accomplished? What's still to come?

2. Write it all out: Create a spreadsheet or some other type of document that lists your five-year goals one by one.

3. Now create sublists under each entry that detail the steps you have to take en route to that goal. List them in order, with estimated time spans appended that take into consideration any factors of your life that need to be worked in. Denote each factor as either within your power to control, not within your power to control, or unknown at this time.

4. As part of this five-year plan, set both short-term and long-term goals to enact it—set daily, weekly, monthly, and yearly goals that reinforce the plan.

5. Regularly schedule reviews of this written plan to track goal attainment and monitor progress—say, on the third Sunday of every month.

6. Make adjustments to the details of the plan/goals as needed.

7. Share your written plan with someone close to you who will help hold you accountable for making your vision a reality by following your plan!

Be Prudent

Human characteristics run the gamut. Some bring us closer to the dark, like jealousy, envy, resentment, anger, and dishonesty; and some are life-affirming, in that they bring us more and more into the light, where it's easier to seed and sustain the kind of mindset of positivity that we're after. Prudence is one such life-affirming, light-bearing trait we should all strive to possess.

As we've discussed, the negative inner critic feeds on negative, unpleasant experiences, some of which are externally caused and some of which are internally caused. Ultimately, however, as I've tried to make plain from page one, we are the authors of our own fates, regardless of circumstances that have inhabited our lives. We cannot eradicate the existence or impact of these circumstances, but we can rewire our brains to rewrite them in such a way that they become moments of learning for us instead of just memories of pain and hardship. One can choose to follow in a parent's footsteps by adopting the same self-destructive habits they saw modeled in their childhood home, or one can do a complete about-face and choose to run, not walk, in the exact opposite direction. That's why two children can be reared in the same household, and one can go on to win a Nobel Prize while and the other can face jail time. On what basis? On the basis of their choices. And, as a general rule at least, good choices, the best choices, are made with prudence.

Prudence is the capacity to think and act intentionally and thoughtfully using the tools of reason, discipline, shrewdness, and good judgment. Prudence keeps us safe by cautioning us against threats and leading us away from danger. Prudence makes wise use of resources, maximizing our potential in all areas of life, such as time management, relationship-building, career growth, and mental and physical health. When we are prudent, we are careful with our words and our actions. We value ourselves and we live by our values.

In terms of finances, prudence means the ability to spend wisely, live within one's means, and save for rainy days. To be prudent with time is to aim to use every minute of every hour of every day productively. To be prudent with health is to exercise regularly, eat well, get sufficient sleep, and schedule regular checkups. To be prudent with your decision-making is to actively resolve to make the best possible choices you can at any given time and in any given circumstance, informed by your visions, your principles, and your ethics. To be prudent in life means no less than to live wisely and well, to enhance your growth and development, and to use your strengths and sensibilities to handle whatever life throws at you.

Prudence is within anyone's reach. It is not something you either are or are not born with—it is a habit that you can most assuredly establish and practice daily to improve your life in myriad ways. As you do, you will choose excellence over excuses, honesty over lies, and calmness over anxiety. In the process, your voice of positivity will get louder and louder, overpowering the negativity that is constantly warring for supremacy over the mind.

Be Responsible

Responsibility is just a fact of life—it comes with the territory. People can shirk responsibility, true, but in the end, it's going to rest in *somebody's* lap. When you're born, your parents are responsible for your survival, nurturance, and growth. Society also places the responsibility on them for your education, your moral grounding, your knowledge of right and wrong, and your behaviors out in public and in communal spaces. When you misbehave or make mistakes as a child, your parents are held responsible. But as you grow, the responsibility shifts to you, and by the time you're an adult, you're fully responsible for yourself. If you commit offenses, society demands that you answer for your actions.

Everyone knows this, right? This is evident, wouldn't you agree? And yet people very often ignore their responsibilities. Despite the fact that irresponsibility is a social crime; people commit it with alarming frequency. Every time someone has unprotected sex, it is irresponsible—every single time. The chances of getting pregnant or contracting an STD rise to 100% if you do it often enough. It's only a matter of time before one of these outcomes occurs.

Every hit-and-run, even if it's just a fender-bender ... every instance of shoplifting, even if it's just a pack of gum ... every flirty text to someone who is not your mate ... every occurrence of lazy parenting when you know better ... every time you cheat on a test or lie on a form or shift the burden of blame for something you did onto someone else—each is an act of willful irresponsibility. Some trespasses are graver than others. Adults in a position of authority have been known to take advantage of minors—just turn on the Bravo or Lifetime or True Crime channel and you'll find real-life stories of teacher, coaches, and other mentors who have taken sexual advantage of boys and girls. On the other side of the spectrum are lesser infractions that we let ourselves off the hook for: chunks of text copied off the Internet for a college paper we didn't get done in time; letting our boss believe that great idea was ours when it wasn't; buying that pair of shoes when we know we're going to come up short on our credit card bill this month.

Don't be that person—that person who takes some kind of shortcut that will only lead to coming up short on yourself eventually. To compromising your integrity. To being ashamed of yourself. To digging the hole deeper with every chosen instance of irresponsibility over responsibility. A friend once told me that the first aid kit sits next to the body bag. What starts as a minor injury can blossom into life-threatening, soul-crushing danger.

Stay away from the danger from the start by living according to the values that have been ingrained in you, if not by your upbringing, then by society at large. Steer away from temptations, habits, behaviors, and people who can lead you astray and stay the course of honesty, compassion, righteousness, and goodness. It's easier to stay on the right path all along than it is to get back on it once you've seriously detoured, so choose to be responsible and do the right thing if you want an easier, smoother, more peaceful ride through life. Even if you're responsible for the wrong reasons—like a man who doesn't cheat on his wife, not because he loves her, but only because he's afraid of the social and professional ramifications of getting caught—that's fine. You're still showing respect for yourself, for others in your life, and for the consequences you will inevitably face—someday, in some way—if you make thoughtless, careless, reckless decisions.

An oak tree cannot birth a banana, and a banana tree cannot bear an oak. When you sow negativity, irresponsibility, and mediocrity in your life, you will get the same in return. It may take a while for your past to come back to haunt you, but it will. Just watch the news—all the political and entertainment icons who've had their careers come to a screeching end and are actually facing criminal charges because of abuses they committed as long as decades ago.

Be a responsible citizen, a responsible worker, a responsible human being. When you can be proud of your choices and actions, you leave little room for the voice of negativity to creep in and shame you, and you instead create more room for the voice of positivity to praise and applaud your worthy efforts.

Be Accountable

Show me a person who has suffered an eventual and horrible fall, and I'll show you someone who didn't think they were accountable to anybody. A notable Christian speaker once said he was approached by three young women after a seminar. They wanted to know the one-character trait in a man they should be on the lookout for. He said, "A man must be teachable."

When you are accountable, you put yourself under the direct oversight of a few people. You do this not because you fear them, but because you respect them. A woman who is accountable to her husband will stop smoking because he doesn't like it. She won't stop because she fears him. He will not physically harm her. She will stop because she loves and values this man—and even if she doesn't stop completely all at once, she will gradually find a way to succeed in her pledge to quit in order to be accountable to the sanctity of her marriage.

Some people just don't care, though. They don't feel beholden to anyone. They fear no one. They cannot be advised, they cannot be taught, they cannot be corrected. Why? Because they are always right or they are completely self-centered. They do not acknowledge things greater than them and above them. They are stubborn, dogged, intractable, and self-righteous to a fault. These are some of the hardest folks to provide counseling to! When you try to press them to align with generally accepted expectations, they take it personally and walk away from therapy. I find this to be a pitiable way to live—to think you owe nothing and no one anything. Life is simply yours for the living, any way you choose, even if it hurts others.

It's good to be accountable to others—your friends, your coworkers, your fellow committee members—but most important is to be accountable to yourself. That means that even when there's no one there watching you, you do the right thing *for yourself*. This is the highest form of accountability. Set your own rules and abide by them, even when there's no one there to reprimand you if you misstep. Hold yourself accountable by setting your personal standards high and then respecting and loving yourself enough to perpetually maintain those standards.

Be accountable to your family as well, your kids. Why should you be accountable to your kids? Well, you're responsible for them, and decisions you make can significantly impact not just their present, but their future. When you are accountable to your children, you'll think twice before using the family home as collateral on a bank loan for an untested business idea. When you are accountable to your family, you will do everything in your power to protect them, not just yourself. When you're lured by power, wealth, fame, or pleasures of the flesh, you'll think twice and not take actions that will be detrimental to their lives. I remember a Bible verse that goes, "A good man leaves an inheritance for his children's children." You are planting seeds with your life that will bear fruit for generations to come—be aware of that and recognize the power of your own self-accountability. Each time you do, you turn up the volume of the positive voice in your mind because you're someone who can hold your head high and show up for others and for yourself.

The five steps outlined above will build the positivity in your life—there's no doubt about that. Accepting who you are, setting a vision, a plan, and goals for yourself, and consciously choosing to be prudent, responsible, and accountable in your daily actions and interactions are clear ways to a healthier and happier existence. They may sound like commonsense ideas that any rational person would follow, but when the negative inner critic has a grip on us, we tend to underestimate common sense and overestimate criticism and complaints. Conflicts of the mind exist—they are real and true and deep. But you hold the megaphone of your life. Are you going to allow the booing to take center stage, or are you going to choose to concentrate on the cheering? Strengthening the inner critic's voice of positivity will allow you to drop the curtain on the darkness behind you and walk into the spotlight.

CHAPTER 8

Exercises to Combat Negative Thought Processes

Empty your mind, be formless, shapeless—like water. Now you put water into a cup, it becomes the cup, you put water into a bottle, it becomes the bottle, you put it in a teapot, it becomes the teapot. Now water can flow or it can crash. Be water, my friend.

—Bruce Lee

If you've been following along with this book with your journal at your side and have made the recommended entries in it, you not only probably already have a good understanding of your inner voices by now, but you've probably also already made some good progress reining them in and taming them within your control. At least I hope so!

The handful of exercises in this chapter are intended to keep that progress going, now and well into the future. I haven't reinvented the wheel here—these are just some long-established and well-accepted techniques to modify behavior and enhance consciousness. Self-growth should be and hopefully is a lifelong pursuit for you. All of these approaches can be applied to any area of growth you're working on and can make that work all the more focused and effective.

If you've come this far on the journey with me, please take these last few steps. They seem simple, maybe something you don't think you have time for. Very often, however, the simple route is the one that holds the most direct answers, so engage in these exercises and see what they unlock in you.

Exercise #1: Personal Thoughts

It seems an opportune time to clarify and summarize the insights you're taking away from this book. In your journal or on your computer, write your responses to the following prompts, and then see if any of your answers lead you to new thoughts, additional insights, or any other observations worth noting.

1. Of the three voices of your inner critic—the negative voice, the positive voice, and the voice of objectivity—which is the strongest in you right now at this point in your life, which is the loudest?

2. Why? What does that voice say to you most often?

3. If you had to summarize what each of the three voices says to you most often—in just a sentence or two—what would it be?

4. Which of those messages are helpful and which are harmful? Why?

5. Name three things you can do to counter and combat the harmful ones.

6. Name your top three goals in life right now. Next to each, write down a step you will commit to taking in the next thirty days to make progress in that area.

7. When your inner voice tells you you can't do something, despite what you know are your best intentions and best efforts, *why* is it telling you this goal is out of your reach?

What's the reasoning you hear in your brain blocking your way? Is the message true—is it really?—or is this an excuse or explanation based on fear of failing?

8. How have you applied some of the information in this book to your professional life?

9. How have you applied some of the information in this book to your personal life?

10. Is it working? If so, what do you need to continue to do? If not, what do you need to start doing?

Exercise #2: Mindfulness

Simply put, mindfulness means being fully aware of and grounded in the present moment—the ability to bring your awareness to what you're experiencing, sensing, doing, and thinking in the current moment. When you learn to situate yourself completely in the present, even for very short periods of time, it's much easier to ignore the lingering pains of the past and to quell the anxieties of the future. When you're more tuned in to your senses, your mind is less available to get caught up in well-worn loops and grooves that keep you stuck in old, useless patterns.

The best thing about mindfulness is that as you train your brain to be more mindful, you can actually alter the physical structure of the brain—it's like a remodel where you learn to rearrange things such that positive and proactive elements of your cognitive processes are accentuated at the forefront while flaws and deficits can recede more into the background.

Mindfulness is something that is available to all of us—of any age, background, cultural heritage, or education level. It's a God-given universal resource that you can learn to tap into whenever you set your mind to it (pun intended), particularly when you need a break from the inner critic's negative voice pestering you. This is a very individual, solitary practice that you and you alone commit to to help yourself live a more productive, balanced, peaceful life.

As such, on your own, whenever you have a free span of time, particularly when you're going through something mentally taxing, do an Internet search for "mindfulness" and visit at least three websites on the topic that capture your interest. Don't click on any ads or purchase any products or feel pressured to do anything other than read up on mindfulness and, as you do so, consider how and when this utterly free, completely accessible learned skill can help you.

1. List or bookmark three websites you found useful and would like to return to.
2. Choose at least one activity or recommendation from each website to try.
3. Do another search for "mindfulness" on YouTube and, based on their length and content, choose at least three videos to watch on the practice.
4. Follow along with the videos and do what's instructed.
5. Now choose just one mindfulness step you will incorporate into your routine every day for a week for a total of one month—choose one step for week one, a second step for week two, and so on.
6. At the end of each week, when you've tried out that mindfulness activity at least once a day every day, record in your journal how it felt, how it did (or did not) affect you as you were doing it, what you liked (or did not like) about the process.
7. At the end of the month-long experiment, write about it in detail: what you learned, how starting to practice mindfulness changed your daily life, what you'd like to take from it going forward, how you think you can benefit from certain mindfulness practices.

8. Now pay it forward by sharing your new experience with someone else close to you—tell them what you tried and why and invite them to either practice with you or on their own.

Exercise #3: Meditation

Meditation is the perfect complement to mindfulness. Whereas mindfulness sharply and acutely focuses the lens of your mind on something right in front of you in your physical existence, meditation purposely clouds that lens to free your mind of constant and counterproductive tendencies that sap you of more healthful and peaceful energies. Both practices aim to slow you down: slow your thoughts, slow your heartbeat, slow the hecticness and chaos of daily life, taking a breather from your regular regimen of work and chores and family obligations to devote some self-care to your brain, body, mind, and spirit. Both intend to lead you to more clarity, calmness, and stability. To me, though, the difference lies between focusing your mind, on the one hand, versus clearing your mind, on the other. With mindfulness, you hold on to one single sensation at a time—like what the cube of watermelon in your mouth feels like, its temperature, its texture, its taste, the sounds in your ears when you bite into it. Really zoning in on that bit of fruit, to be extraordinarily aware of what you're engaged in at that present moment. With meditation, you're attempting to zone out, to let go.

There is no right or wrong way to meditate. Again, I'm going to challenge you to undertake some self-guided research online and experiment with meditation based on what you discover. Goodness knows you'll find lots of different opinions and approaches: Some meditation teachers have you mentally repeat one mantra so that all other words leave your consciousness; some try to lead you to empty your mind entirely. Some advocate complete silence and a blanket of darkness in a quiet corner of your home; others endorse background music or white noise to retune your mind while enjoying sunlight shining down on you outside somewhere. Some lead guided meditations with their voice; others leave you to your own devices. Some recommend sitting; some invite you to lie down.

You probably know what's coming? Yep, just as you did for mindfulness, I want you to do a search for "meditation" online and follow a few reputable-looking links that speak to you. Don't accept my explanation of what meditation is or is not—decide for yourself after you've studied up on it a bit. Then embark on another month-long experiment (at a minimum) of introducing yourself to meditation, any way you want, anytime you want, for stints as long as you want. Some pointers:

- There's no need to buy supplies or spend money. You can find a plethora of free videos and audio recordings online so you can try out different approaches. If you find a specific series or leader that strongly appeals to you, by all means you can purchase a subscription or an app, but it's not necessary to enjoy the benefits of meditation. YouTube has great videos such as rainforest sounds that you can listen to while you are in deep mediation. I often use rainforest sounds in my private practice with clients as I am working with them through *guided mediations* to reduce anxiety.

- Pick a time each day to do your daily meditation. You're much more likely to stick with it if you've mapped out a few minutes per day at the same time, so it becomes part of your schedule. Some people prefer first thing in the morning, some people find it relaxes them right before bed—whatever time works best for you is the right time.

- Meditate at least once a day. If you prefer to break it up into two fifteen-minute sessions or three ten-minute sessions, that's great too. But aim for at least once a day, in an effort to form a new habit.

- Find a place in your home where you can meditate alone and undisturbed and designate that as your meditation space. Little by little, add things to this space to heighten the effectiveness of your practice, like a scented candle or a blanket to warm you or a yoga block to sit on to support your posture. Make arrangements with anyone you live with that will give you peace and quiet in this space during your meditation sessions.

- Start small. Find a few five-minute sessions and begin with them. At first, you'll just be trying to be still that long and detach for that long. Then, a few days later, try eight-minute stints ... then ten ... then twenty. Some people find that it takes them longer to get to the mental state they're hoping to achieve; others take to meditation quite quickly and just as quickly learn to access the part of their brain they're trying to target.

- Don't give up! If you have trouble quieting your mind or letting go of distractions and anxieties while you meditate, that's okay! That's normal—most people do not find it at all natural to try to empty their brain and just sign off and zone out during waking hours. Just stick with it—it's doing you good even if you can't actually feel a difference. Your brain knows you're flexing its muscles in new ways, and that's all that matters for now.

After you've practiced meditation for several weeks or a month, jot down in your journal:

- What does and does not work for you?
- What time of day is most available to you for regular meditation?
- What did you find easiest to adjust to?
- What are you finding most challenging?
- What kinds of thoughts, feelings, and sensations surface during your practice?
- Have you yet achieved a state of "letting go," or is this still a work in progress?

- What did you get from this experiment? Has it been worth it so far?
- Do you think you'll continue meditating? If so, what kind of commitment are you willing to make right now to make meditation part of your daily life?

Exercise #4: Relaxation

Okay, this one is easier than meditation, I promise! Relaxation is exactly that—just engaging in purely enjoyable activities (or doing nothing at all, actually) that allow you to completely forget about your worries and obligations for a while so that your body and mind can become calm. When they do, your soul will follow. This is one important component of self-care.

You're not necessarily going for anything here, like achieving positivity or focusing your consciousness or reaching a state of detachment. You are just resting. All of you is resting. And each person will find that rest and relaxation in different ways: taking a walk in nature, sunbathing on the beach, reading a good book, escaping into a good movie, cooking, cleaning, painting, building, listening to music, cuddling with your cat on the couch, taking a bath, rocking your baby to sleep. Relaxation can be as simple as slouching in front of the TV with a big bowl of popcorn in your lap or as varied as taking a trip to someplace exotic and ziplining through the wilderness. We all need breaks—especially when we're doing the hard work of self-growth—to recuperate from previous exertions and replenish our mind, body, and soul for what comes next.

What do you do to relax? What do you find fills your soul with happiness, contentment, and peace and energizes you to get back up and do it all over again, as well as you can? It's imperative that you're aware of things you can do and places you can go—mental or otherwise—to refill your tank when it's running low.

Jot down at least five things that relax you. Next to each, write down why you think they relax you—if you identify a common thread, like doing something creative or doing something that grounds you in your body, you'll be able to extend that realization into other areas and times in your life, to bring you more peace at particularly stressful times. Lastly, assign a time in the next two weeks to engage in each of these five things. For example, if you love to soak in your hot tub, schedule a soak for Sunday night at 7:30 p.m., to end your weekend on a positive note and set the tone for a reenergized Monday morning.

1.

2.

3.

4.

5.

Exercise #5: Exercise!

Now it's time to do the complete opposite: Get your body up and moving! Not only does physical activity get you out of your head, but it's just downright good for you. When your body is supple and limber, you feel freer, lighter, and more flexible in all ways; you breathe easier and you can think more clearly. One of my clients is a writer. Whenever she hits an obstacle in a project, can't find the words or see a solution to a problem, she swears a brisk walk, a visit to the gym, or even stretching in a hot shower unblocks the block and guides her directly to the answer she was fruitlessly searching for at her desk.

Consistent exercise boosts your confidence and, in turn, your positivity. Negative thought processes, in contrast, gain strength when one is idle, troubled, or sick. Regular exercise soothes a troubled mind, boosts immunity, and generally improves health.

If you're new to exercise or have any health issues, you'll obviously want to be careful and mindful, perhaps talking to your physician about a beginner program. If you're already a regular exerciser, kick things up a notch to push you out of a funk or give you an injection of added energy—take a forty-five-minute yoga class instead of a half hour, add some speed or incline to the treadmill, try out some HIIT at the gym or in your backyard, incorporate some sprints into your regular jog. And no matter what shape you're in, don't forget to warm up before every session. We can't create new injuries in your body when you're trying to heal old injuries in your mind!

Write down five exercises you will commit to doing/trying over the course of the next two weeks, and next to each, schedule a slot to do them so you actually make it happen. For example, if you know Wednesdays are your long days because of your son's weekly Scouts meeting, don't set up the unrealistic expectation of swimming laps that day. Instead, book a date with a friend to visit the Y on Saturday morning or schedule a walk with your spouse for Monday after work.

1.

2.

3.

4.

5.

Exercise #6: Positive Self-Talk

Here's another simple but highly effective exercise that does wonders to eradicate negative thought processes. Create a sheet of paper that looks like the sample below. Leave blanks to fill in at different times and make copies so you can reuse positive self-talk, affirmations and statements over and over. Cut some pages into strips and tuck them in places where you'll see them often; tack a sheet to the bulletin board in your office or affix it to the fridge. Jot down a few of the statements on Post-it Notes and adhere them to your computer screen or mirror or car dashboard.

The important part is to compose positive messages to yourself that you can read and repeat daily. You can even put a bunch of them in a jar and pull one before each meditation session. That can be your mantra for the entire meditation session—just that one statement over and over for ten minutes: *I am beautiful.* Or *My soul is beautiful.* Or *My mind is open to new possibilities.* Use these prompts or create some of your own. The possibilities are literally limitless.

I am *smart* _____.
I am *intelligent* _____.
I am _____.
I am _____.
I am _____.
I am _____.
My soul is _____.
My mind is _____.
My spirit is _____.
I can _____.
I will _____.
I will not _____.
I have the power to _____.
I am capable of _____.

I will forgive _____.
I am committed to _____.
I am wonderful at _____.
My superpower is _____.
Today will be _____.

CHAPTER 9

Conclusion:
Letting Go to Let in Growth

You shall know the truth, and the truth shall make you free.
—Jesus Christ

The Talmud says, "We do not see things the way they are. We see things the way we are." I know of no truer statement—nor one more pertinent to the enterprise of encouraging people to discover who they are at their deepest, purest, most authentic cores. To discover why they think and act in certain ways and how they can then change the thoughts and behaviors over which they have control and accept and forgive those over which they do not.

We all have an inner critic inside us. All of us. No one is immune. More often than not, we attend to and heed the messages that emanate from the negative aspect of this critic. The negative critic tries to trap us into focusing on the shortcomings in our lives—what we don't have, what we lack, what we are not, what others seem to possess beyond our reach. It wants us to continue replaying negative feedback in our minds in a constant loop of self-criticism, self-doubt, and denial of our capabilities because then we find justification for the very shortcomings it keeps pointing out. We can assign blame. Sometimes to others, mostly to ourselves.

Is this pattern serving you? Or is it holding you back, a little or a lot? Because we all have a negative critic on our shoulder whispering in our ear day and night, we must all find a way to either quiet that voice, correct that voice, or defeat that voice so that we can go on with our lives, for the very short time we have here on the planet to do so, as healthfully, happily, and harmoniously as we can.

The negative inner critic is only one of the voices in your head, only one of the players on your mental stage, and you cannot let it play the starring role very often or for very long. If you do, you accept its power over you, you relinquish control to it, and you live your life at half-mast, never flying as high and proud as you could because you live in constant fear of its criticism, limitations, and judgments.

The path to relegating the negative critic to just a supporting player in your story (if not just some cameo appearances!) is self-acceptance. Not self-aggrandizement. Not self-adoration and self-idolization. Not prioritizing yourself above everyone and everything else. Just acceptance—of where you came from, of the influences that molded you, of the past experiences that shaped you, of the people who tried their best but nevertheless often failed in loving and supporting you. Accepting what was then and what is now. Accepting that you're never going to be a beauty queen or a rocket scientist or a Pulitzer Prize winner, but that you can be beautiful, gifted, and an absolute treasure to the family and friends you choose to surround yourself with now.

The way to self-acceptance is understanding ourselves as best we can. We might never get to a point of complete understanding, but we owe it to ourselves to spend at least part of our lives coming to terms with who we are, who we were born to be, and who we want to become if we're to have true, meaningful, deep connections with others and with our environments. We can be gentler on ourselves without absolving ourselves of all wrong. We can feel more important and valuable by assigning a little less importance and value to struggles that belong in our rearview mirror, no longer monopolizing our vision out the much more expansive windshield in front of us. When we have a deeper understanding of ourselves and take a less harsh view of the reality of our lives, this creates a greater sense of intimacy with the person we are and the people we want to share our lives with.

We are not perfect, we have flaws. Who says life was supposed to be a cakewalk filled with only happy smiles and ideal relationships and overflowing bank accounts and jobs handed to us on a silver platter? Do you think you'd have a resilient nature and a courageous soul if you never had to earn anything the hard way? Where would the growth be in that? Where would be the irreplaceable learning and development of character, integrity, nobility, and loyalty? Growing up in the hood, poverty, a broken home, abusive father, distant mother, favoritism, cancer, death, divorce, all made you who you are today.

Yes, we are flawed, and we have hardships, and there are some problems we will face that are not easily resolved. But we are more than our hatful of problems; we are not the by-products of them—they are the by-products of what we do not yet know about ourselves, what we do not yet have dominion over, what we have not yet learned to master. And turning down the volume of your inner negative voice and turning up the volume of your inner positive voice *is* something you can master.

Remember: You are the author of your own story. If you opt to write yourself as a victim, you will play the role of the victim in your life's story. If you opt to write yourself as a hero, you will be a hero. Somewhere in between lies the average human being: the protagonist. The protagonist does not need to perform great feats or overcome great odds like saving the damsel in distress or slaying the mighty dragon. The protagonist is just responsible for keeping the story going, for maintaining intentional momentum, and for actively participating in the plotline as it advances toward its intended destination. If you can do all that—if you accept the role of being the protagonist of your own play and directing its trajectory—you are far more than an average human being.

You have something to offer the world. You do. So isn't it time that you get out of your own way and be active in fulfilling your purpose in life, letting go of the often-self-imposed leashes that keep you tethered to patterns and processes that are stalling your odyssey instead of stimulating it? Yes, it's time! The minute you decide to adjust the knobs in your brain and listen to positive messages more than you listen to negative ones, you're making better use of your time and your God-given gifts, every single moment of every single day.

Guideposts Along the Way

By now, you've hopefully come to the decision to try a new way, to redirect your path so you can stop falling into the same old potholes and detours that have hampered the progress you want to make in your self-development. Well, that's about the best thing you can do for yourself—and it isn't going to benefit just you. I promise that if you take the steps outlined in this book, your life will become more promising and more fulfilling beyond the confines of your own inner world, deepening and enriching your relationships and interactions with others as well.

But trying new things is hard. Making progress doesn't come easy. You will meet resistance, both internal and external, when you start behaving in unfamiliar ways with familiar people, when you try to break out of a set shape that's grown comfortable if not all that helpful and try to reset the mold of your own life. You may have to make some difficult decisions. We've been talking about things like changing careers, having tough conversations with people who intimidate you, removing yourself from unhealthy situations, maybe from an unhappy marriage to the wrong partner. Saying no to abuse. How will you know if you're doing the right things for the right reasons? How will you know if you're just being selfish or self-serving as opposed to truly making inroads with some ongoing inner conflicts that have been plaguing you?

Well, there is no one pat answer—"truth" can be an elusive ideal to uncover, and "right" and "wrong" often aren't clear absolutes. We head back into that gray area we discussed earlier when we recognize that what is "right" and what is "wrong" depends, sometimes greatly, on what any particular individual *thinks* is right or wrong. In the end, you're the only one who can enact the decisions you make and you're the one who has to live with the consequences.

When you're at a crossroads like that, trying to navigate the kinds of difficult choices we've been talking about in this book, there are some guideposts you can follow to help you discern if you're basing your decisions on the right considerations, heading in the right direction, and making the best choices for you and your surrounding community as you aim to approach the truth as closely as possible and walk the honorable path toward resolving the *conflicts of the mind.*

Conscience

We know that the mind is the seat of our conscious being. And as the language implies, our consciousness houses our conscience. Mostly, the conscience skews toward the positive—rightfully cautioning us against taking certain steps that are morally questionable—and it might just be the closest thing to "truth" we can access.

So listen to it. When your conscience says, *Don't do that—don't steal that ink cartridge from work; don't throw her under the bus to save my own hide; don't skip Tasha's soccer game to go grab a drink with the guys*—heed that higher voice. Do you remember the comic Flip Wilson saying, "The devil made me do it"? Well, your conscience is the flip side of that voice that says, "I just couldn't do it. My mind wouldn't let me." We give ourselves over to the power of our minds all the time, talk ourselves into why we're allowed to do something we know we shouldn't. Better to put the power of the mind to more beneficial use, talking ourselves out of what our higher self already knows would be a misstep.

When you are about to take an action, if your conscience nags you against it, rethink it. You can always change your mind and proceed with something iffy, but you can't undo something once it's been done. You can't unhurt someone once you've hurt them. There might not be hard-and-fast absolutes in this world as to what's "right" and what's "wrong," but there are commonly accepted standards of "good" and "bad" that we know and recognize in our gut. When you go against that, you create cognitive dissonance. There's already enough dissonance out there in the world; don't add to it by making more of your own. As Jiminy Cricket said to Pinocchio, "Let your conscience be your guide."

Growth

If you're confused about where a life decision might lead you, ask yourself if the likely outcome for you is one of slipping backward, maintaining the status quo, or generating some type of growth. You want to shoot for curtain number three. Being open-minded, inquisitive, and curious leads to growth; being fearful, untrusting, and closed-minded, set in your ways, leads to stagnation.

It's fine to hold fast to religious and cultural beliefs and traditions that contribute to your sense of yourself and your place in the world, but relying too heavily on dogma and theories can restrain the mind and keep it captive. Being open to new ideas doesn't mean blind acceptance of any novel belief that comes your way. But room for growth is made when we begin to see things in a different light, to let in different perspectives. As we grow, our minds pick through all we're exposed to and distinguish fact from fiction. But we can't weigh varied and possibly conflicting ideas unless we're first open enough to learn about them and explore the effects they may have. The learning itself *is* the growth.

Knowledge

Ignorance of the outcomes of your decisions doesn't save you from the consequences of them, does it? There's only so far that "I didn't know" will take you. Make it your duty to know, or at least to try to get to know. Examine things, analyze and deduce and reason and assess—don't just take the lazy way out by choosing to do something and then saying, "Oops. That was a mistake. I should have thought that out more." Think it out beforehand.

Knowledge is always good; knowledge always trumps oblivion. Knowledge, as they say, is power. Read books, watch educational videos, listen to lectures, ask people you respect for guidance and advice. Study, research, investigate. When it's time to make decisions in your life, you'll want them to be informed decisions, not knee-jerk reactions based on short-sighted desires. When you're playing the long game, using knowledge as a tool to get where you want to go will only lead to more knowledge. Be a perpetual student of life. That's the only way you're going to get to the head of the class.

Lawfulness

The philosopher Thomas Hobbes had a pessimistic view of humanity and called the life of man "nasty, brutish, and short." He felt that humans would run rampant, allow their selfishness and personal interests to plow all over everything else, if they weren't governed by laws carrying penalties, and so he believed in firm government. I'm not going to go that far, no—I think that most people want to be good and try to be good most of the time … but we can't deny that sometimes humans only do good because we fear the punishment of getting caught for being bad. Especially when we're young and reckless.

It should go without saying, that… Laws are in place to maintain civil order and to protect—to guard us against the trespasses of others and even to guard us against ourselves sometimes. I don't care how much you dream of getting rich, don't fall for get-rich-quick schemes that could swindle people out of money. I don't care how broke you are, don't take a job with a disreputable company that you know targets innocent victims. I don't care how well you did on your chemistry exam or how big of a fight you got in with your mother, don't do things that you know will cause further emotional injury. Don't run out on obligations, don't cheat on your taxes, don't run red lights, and don't flirt with the boundaries of the law.

Sounds like a lot of "don't" lecturing, right? Well, it should just be commonsensical to stay away from danger in life, but sometimes when we're feeling dejected and severely disappointed over the way our lives are going, we make decisions that will almost certainly come back to haunt us later, even if we get away with something shady temporarily.

A bad choice doesn't even have to be illegal or immoral to inflict harm on yourself or someone else. Shooting up heroin is a physical assault upon yourself. Hitting your kid out of anger will leave a mark you will not be able to erase for decades, maybe ever. Ghosting your boyfriend because you don't have the courage to break up with him considerately and conscientiously inflicts unnecessary hurt that you don't want to come back to you later in life. It might not always be easier to do the right thing, but in the long run, you will indeed have an easier life if you walk the righteous path.

Let's all make a pledge to follow the higher laws—those that govern decency and goodness and compassion. If we all abided by the Golden Rule and based our decisions concerning others on how we'd like to be treated ourselves, half the world's problems would be solved. Yes, there may be times when you have to make sensitive decisions that could lead to further difficulties.

As you get more in touch with the inner workings of your inner critic, you'll learn to trust the positive messages more and the negative messages less. When you make a choice that's good for you, your inner critic will know. When you make a choice that's bad for you, your inner critic will know. And when you need to make a choice somewhere in between, call in the voice of objectivity to act as mediator. Befriend all the aspects of the inner critic's voice and you'll have built-in advice and wisdom that will keep you true to yourself and respectful of others.

Cause and Effect

As you go forth in your life with your new knowledge about the voices that drive your behaviors and decision-making, the consequences of your thoughts, actions, and choices will become clearer. The universal law of cause-and-effect states that for every action in the world, there will be a reaction—usually something similar. If you do something loving, it will generate more love as a result (like the grateful smile and hug your sister will give you when you tell her what a great sibling she is). If you want forgiveness from someone, grant forgiveness yourself.

Consequences We don't always know what they will be clearly or immediately, but you can count on them coming down the pike sooner or later. That's why it's of paramount importance to consciously and deliberately weigh the effects of anything we're considering doing and be willing to make the sacrifices it will take to create the outcomes we want. The ability to objectively analyze the impact our actions will likely make can save us from ridicule, shame, pain, defeat, heartache, and struggle.

Someone who lives without thought of consequences will eventually become inconsequential. You reap what you sow. When you sow discord, be prepared for a storm. When you sow disloyalty, be prepared for betrayal. And when you sow kindness, don't be surprised when it comes back to you threefold.

Honesty

The last guidepost to mark your way as you journey to live the life you want is honesty. To get to the root of any matter, an honest appraisal of it is necessary. To build a genuine bond with someone, the relationship must be built on sincerity and truth. To solve a problem, it must be approached openly, candidly, and transparently. When shields and veils block our view of things, honesty cannot prevail.

The most important person to be honest with, of course, is yourself. Even if you fool everyone else around you, you cannot fool yourself. You can try—you can try to talk yourself into things that aren't true, but your inner critic will not let you off the hook that easily. When you're being dishonest, the critic will admonish you, taunt you, and judge you harshly. When it comes to dealing with the types of inner conflicts that beset us all at some point or another, we must find the courage and have the fortitude to learn to see things as they are and say it like it is.

As you incorporate the ideas in this book into your life and start practicing new ways of thinking and acting in the world, know that your route to less negativity and more positivity must be lined with honesty. Be just as honest about your weaknesses as you are about your strengths so you can realistically and effectively address them; and be just as honest with others as you are with yourself. The negative critic will feast on your self-deceit if you allow it to. But starve it of untruths and give voice to the positive critic inside of you.

Learning from the Past and Looking Toward the Future

A young man who had been homeless for years was panhandling on the street for spare change from passersby. One day, a painter stopped in front of the young man. He set up his easel, took out his paints, and started to mark his canvas.

The young man was curious about what the painter was painting.

But the painter took his time and used all the colors on his palette. When he was finally finished with his portrait, he turned it toward the young man. "Tell me what you see," he asked him.

The young man stared at the painting and said, "Well, I see a man who has a smile on his face. He's dressed in a nice suit; his hair is combed; and he looks pretty happy about life."

The painter replied, "That's good. Tell me what else you see."

The young man looked a little closer at the picture. "Well, um …"

"Go on," the painter prompted. "Tell me what you see."

"Well, it can't be," the young man said. "His face looks like mine … but my hair is not combed, I don't have a suit, I'm not happy inside like this man. I don't have a home, I don't have a job to go to, I don't have much to smile about. How could this be me?"

The painter answered, "Son, this is you! I painted you not as you are, but as you can be."

Many of us feel controlled by the past, we feel constrained by the circumstances of where we came from and where we've been. But the past no longer exists. It is no longer here. The people, the places, and the situations of our past are only memories now. Our memories can pave the way into the present—they stay with us—but they are not the full reality, not even the majority of the reality, of the present. And they certainly don't have to control the future.

If you find yourself in a perpetual state of reliving abuse, resentment, anger, if you spend so much time ruminating on the "should haves," you've punished yourself long enough. It is time to face, accept, and embrace the self you are now, your present self, to become more than you've ever been, to become the greatest version of yourself you were meant to be. You have outgrown your past. To truly let it go and allow yourself to move on with what you know now, what you've learned now, who you are now and who you still want to become, you can release your mind from the past. We can achieve true freedom of the mind by growing from your mistakes, self-healing your injuries, and ironing out your complexities.

This doesn't mean we should throw out our pasts like yesterday's garbage, no. Be grateful for the past—for what you've made it through, for the resilience you've shown, for the hard-won lessons you've learned, for all the love you've received and given, for the remarkable, amazing, one-of-a-kind person you've become! Your pen is in your hand, and you could not write your story without the past in which your story began.

The power of the mind—that's the topic we've been sharing. The sometimes-warring, sometimes-complementary, sometimes-balancing factions of the mind that allow to both process and produce a rich and varied inner life that seeps out into our outer existence. Use that power of your mind now to take your past and let it *contribute* to but no longer *control* the story you are writing. Let all parts of you—the good and the not-so-good, the pleasant memories and the more difficult ones, the trials, tribulations, and everything in between—color the chapters of your story with beauty, grace, dignity, gratitude, and clarity. The rest of your story awaits. You can turn the page anytime you want. The end is far from sight and the long road ahead is filled with vast possibilities and unlimited opportunities.

You have greatness inside of you that is waiting to be realized. Every single obstacle that you have experienced has brought you here for such a time as this. You have a greater sense of purpose inside of you just waiting to be released. You were made to be -*you*; you were made for this occasion. All the challenges of your life, all the ups and downs that you have experienced, the trauma, the hard times, the embarrassing moments, have served the purpose of leading you right here. Where you can define yourself, your goals, and your life's path. Take action now by silencing the negative inner critic's voice and transferring power to the positive inner critic instead, to the voice that will propel you towards your dreams and vision for yourself. Now is the time to walk the path that is set before you as you are traveling towards your promise land. Discover the abundance that life has to offer you and just take it! Now is the time to grab hold of the ring of your greatness!

ABRIDGED STYLE SHEET

The Inner Critic
Montriel V. Jamari

Alpha Words/Terms

African American, adj.
aged: school-aged, college-aged
barbed-wire, adj.
Black
coworker
decision-making, n.
Du Bois, W. E. B.
façade
foreign exchange, adj.
goal-setting
goodbye
gray
hunter-gatherer, n.
ingrain
Internet
Jomo Kenyatta International Airport

Kenyan Rift Valley
Kwitone
Mfangano ... Mfangano Island
mindset
people watch, v.
plan-making
problem-solving, n.
savanna
Twa
weaver birds
white

Numbers & Dates

Spell out under 100
1970s
360 BC
eighteen-year-old, n. & adj.
early twenties (age)
five feet one
mid-1940s
Formula 1
three-quarters, n.

Punctuation/Capitalization

Serial comma
No comma with "Jr."
Cap first letter of full statement following a colon

General Comments

Words as words: roman + quotes
Newly introduced/defined terms: italic
Voice of the inner critic: italic (as imagined dialogue, dream speech, or direct thought would be set)

References Used

The Chicago Manual of Style, 17th ed.
www.merriam-webster.com (supplemented/supported by Merriam Webster's Collegiate Dictionary, 11th ed.)

Printed in the United States
by Baker & Taylor Publisher Services